The Chord Scale Theory
& Jazz Harmony

The Chord Scale Theory & Jazz Harmony

BARRIE NETTLES
RICHARD GRAF

Cover Art: 10eg
Layout and music typesetting: T. M. Zentawer
Production: Hans Gruber

Order No. 11216

ISBN 3-89221-056-X

TABLE OF CONTENTS

PREFACE

This book is a guide through Jazz Harmony and Analysis applying contemporary Chord Scale Theory. This method, spread abroad by the Berklee College of Music, is now available – further developed – as a comprehensive textbook for study and private study for the first time. It also considers certain aspects of traditional music and harmony. A review of the harmonic evolution together with examples of the musical literature should help to clarify the genesis of some chords providing a better understanding of contemporary harmony.

While the common use of chord symbols describes chords in isolation only, this book provides a method, which not only identifies a chord's function in relationship to a key but also to other chords. The knowledge about chord structures and vertical analysis is just one aspect of harmony; only a comprehensive understanding of the interrelation of chord changes and the horizontal musical flow provides a deeper appreciation of *moving* music.

The high demands on today's professional musicians require a well-founded insight of the *inner game* of music. This method is reliable for analyzing different idioms of tonal music: jazz, pop, rock, and other contemporary styles; even the analysis of Western art music between 1650 and 1900 gains a new dimension. Enjoy the journey through the world of chord scales and jazz harmony.

ACKNOWLEDGEMENTS

We would like to thank:

- Dr. Bob Myers for reading the American manuscript.
- Steve Rochinski for musical arguments and suggestions.
- Patsy Nettles for being there!

Introduction

JAZZ HARMONY AND TRADITIONAL MUSIC

Jazz – around one hundred years old – is an American art form which developed from the interrelation of African and European music. African music is mainly based on the predominance of melody and dance, which implies accuracy and variety of rhythm. Western art music is distinguished by a highly developed harmony. Both influences were necessary for the birth of jazz.

Spirituals show a direct connection between the harmony of European Protestant music and the black interpretation of melody and rhythm. This phenomenon also occurs in other early jazz styles: Ragtime shows an influence of European marching-music; on the other hand ragtime has inspired classical composers like Claude Debussy or Charles Ives.

But even when jazz had found its own language, the mutual exchange between traditional music and jazz did not stop. Composers soon discovered the potential of blending different styles, rhythmic, and harmonic elements to expand their musical range. The most well-known example of mutual exchange between traditional music and jazz is George Gershwin's "I Got Rhythm," which provides the harmonic structure for "Rhythm Changes" and became an important starting point of the Bebop era. Using elements of jazz was a reason for Gershwin's popularity.

Today, the mutual music exchange is more intense than ever and does not only affect the tonal material but also orchestration and performance: Jazz is no longer exclusively played in night clubs but also on concert stages. On the other hand Western art music tends to incorporate elements of jazz improvisation and orchestration (amplified and electronic instruments).

The interest in Western art music has been growing with each new generation of jazz musicians: Benny Goodman, John Coltrane, Bill Evans, Wynton Marsalis, Keith Jarrett, and many more. (Compare: "Classical Influences on Jazz," Journal of Jazz Studies, Vol. 3 Spring 1976). This had an important effect on jazz harmony and lead to a summary, or even development of the harmonic phenomena of tonal music. A look at the periods of music history and some of its harmonic aspects shows how many traditional elements have been absorbed by jazz:

Modality	Middle Ages to Renaissance 900-1600
Major-minor harmony; sequences and cycle of fifths; four part harmony	Baroque 1600-1750
Emphasis on principal chord functions; dominant seventh chords	Classical 1750-1820
Non-dominant harmony; seventh, ninth chords, chromaticism, chromatic dominants, diminished seventh chords	Romantic 1820-1900
Use of uncommon scales (pentatonic, whole-tone scale...); eleventh, thirteenth chords; constant structures, modality, parallelism, irregular phrases, etc.	Impressionism 1880-1920
Non-diatonic systems, non-functional chords, atonal elements; clusters, sounds; quartal, quintal harmony, etc.	Contemporary

CONTENTS
AND
STRUCTURE

This book is based on the so called Chord Scale Theory. It describes the direct interrelation between chords and scales which do not have independent functions but represent the "two sides of one coin" functioning in relation to a tonal center.

To obtain an understanding of its contents, a chronological study of the entire book is recommended. Advanced readers who study particular chapters have to make sure that technical terms, analytical methods, and symbols are understood and used in the correct meaning. They can be looked up in the appendix but should also be checked by reading previous respectively corresponding chapters. Basic musical knowledge is required for a successful study of this book.

As this harmony proceeds from musical experience, analysis should always be combined with listening and mental sound visualization, so that a chord's sound can be related to its function while reading music reproduces internal, mental sound. Perfect pitch is not necessary. Relative pitch in connection with functional hearing provides an access to music which is more important than a perfect description of pitch. Relative pitch allows the identification of intervals and scale degrees while functional hearing provides perceiving tension and resolution in harmonic progression and relating it to functional categories. Functional hearing and relative pitch are a matter of experience and therefore can be practiced. Improvement of precise hearing and mental sound visualization should accompany the study of this book.

Printed music examples demonstrate practical use, illustrate the text, and should be played on the piano for listening experience. Basic knowledge in piano playing is helpful. This method, as indicated above, was developed from practical application and designed to be used in practice. The term *theory* of chord scales applies only inasmuch as we tried to put different kinds of musical phenomena in a theoretical concept resulting in a publication.

THE EVOLUTION OF HARMONY

The central point of tonal music is **major-minor harmony**. It developed circa 1650 and is still a determinant in music. It is based on the equal tempered tuning, which allows one to transpose and play music in all keys. In connection with the development of the major scale a new harmony was formed.

SCALES

A BRIEF HISTORY

The music of the Middle Ages until the Renaissance (from 800 to 1600) used **modal scales**, also called **church modes** (mode = key, mood). In church music they remained relevant until around 1700.

The names of modal scales have been adopted from the ancient Greeks. Since the 9th century, the plainchant modes have been associated occasionally with the Greek tribal names: Dorian, Phrygian, etc. But through a misinterpretation and a mistake in the tradition they were related to the scales incorrectly. Therefore, the Dorian mode of the Middle Ages, for instance, has nothing to do with the ancient Dorian scale.

The period from about 1400 to 1600, also called the Renaissance, is characterized by an increased interest in studying classical antiquity.

Franchino Gaffurio (1451-1522) revived the Greek names in his **"Practica musice"** (Milan, 1496).

In the theoretical work **"Dodekachordon"** (Basel, 1547) **Heinrich Glarean** (1488-1563) believed to have reconstructed the modal system of the ancient Greeks. For the first time he introduced the Aeolian mode, associated to the root A, and the Ionian mode, associated to the root C. This was the basis for major-minor harmony.

In **"Le Institutioni Harmoniche"** (Venice, 1558) **Gioseffo Zarlino** (1517-1590) describes the "modern modes" very different from the Greek modes, which were named after ancient peoples according to their specific culture, and embracing metrical considerations, affective contents, typical instruments, and instrumental accompaniment. Modern modes rely only on melodic and harmonic factors. Zarlino organized the basis for triadic harmony through classifying all chords as major and minor.

The essential **concept of modal scales** and their names used today traces back to Glarean.

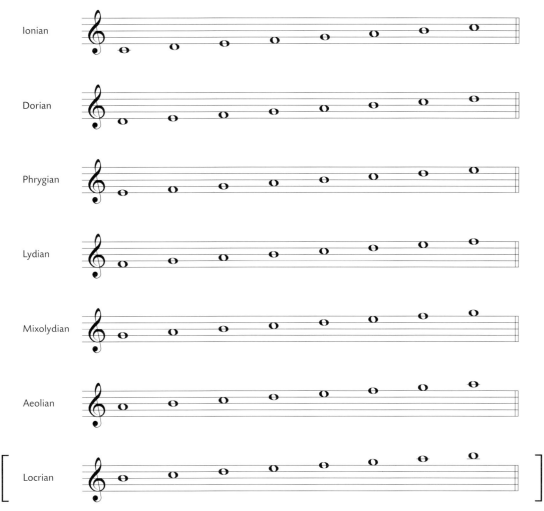

Ionian

Dorian

Phrygian

Lydian

Mixolydian

Aeolian

Locrian

Locrian had never been used in traditional music, because of its structure containing an unstable tonic chord (diminished 5th)

The starting tone and tonal center of these scales (authentic scales) is at the bottom of the range. In traditional practice this pitch is called the **Final**. To meet the registers of voices, additional complementary modes (plagal scales, a fourth below the authentic scales) were used. Although the range changed, the Final was still the same. Because of today's equal tempered tuning system, modes can be transposed.

The application of church modes in contemporary music, and in this book, consider only the Final = tonal center, and not the scale's range. Therefore a distinction between authentic and plagal is not necessary.

The church modes formed the basis for nearly all Western music until 1650, 1700 for sacred music. Consequently, major-minor harmony followed the modes and predominated the next 150 years. The term "tonal music" refers to this period. In the late nineteenth century a revived interest in church modes was a reaction to the chromatic saturation of the dominant oriented music.

Note: For most of this book (except the chapter *Modal Systems*, which shows contemporary use of modality) modal and other scales are used in a functional, not in a modal context. Therefore the term church modes is avoided.

HARMONY

A BRIEF HISTORY

The history of harmony started with doubling a single vocal line (unison and in octave). This appearance is natural to the different register of men and women, but it is far away from any chordal thinking.

In the Middle Ages a fifth (sometimes a fourth) was added to get a richer sound. This style is called **organum**. In the overtone series, the fifth is the next perfect interval after unison and octave. So it was still a kind of doubling.

During the time from about 1450 till 1600 (Renaissance period), harmony was a result of the combination of melodic lines and their consonant or dissonant relationship. So it was different from what we call harmony today.

As mentioned already **Gioseffo Zarlino** (1517-1590) was the first who classified all chords as major and minor ("Le Institutioni Harmoniche," Venice 1558). This was the basis for triadic harmony.

Around 1600, the triad, built by superimposing two thirds, was already established and the main musical device. Chords built by superimposing a third and a fourth, to which we refer today as first inversion, was another but less common chord structure. At this time the concept of accompanying a melody with chords was developed: **Thoroughbass or Figured Bass**.

This system was employed throughout the Baroque period (1600 - 1750). The keyboard player was expected to perform the accompaniment from a part consisting only of a bass line and some additional symbols (numbers) indicating the intervals to be played. When figured bass was first developed, the theory of chord roots and inversions had not been established. Therefore the chord was formed by the description of two intervals above a given bass note. Mostly four voices were played, which required the doubling of one note.

Just as the figured bass system assumes specific knowledge about voice leading, symbols used in jazz and related music require knowledge about harmony and chord scales.

Jean-Philippe Rameau (1683-1764) one of the great theorists of the 18th century established the basic concept for today's functional analysis and coined the names for the primary chords: tonic, subdominant and dominant. In "Traité de l'harmonie" (1722), he discusses the inversion of chords. This was an improvement of the musical harmonic approach and influenced later theoretical writings. From that time, chords were traced back to their initial position: the root position. They were named and analyzed proceeding from their basis – the root.

Hugo Riemann (1849-1919) reorganized and developed Rameau's system of three chord groups to a comprehensive method. In his book about harmony (1880) he introduced new symbols to analyze tonal chord progressions. His concept of harmony is known as functional harmony, because each group has certain characteristics and tendencies in the interplay of a chord progression. The simplified essence of functional harmony is the categorization of three groups of chords, which are known as tonic, subdominant and dominant. Every diatonic chord is assigned to one of these groups. While the tonic represents the most stable center of a tonal progression, the dominant has the strongest tendency for a resolution to the tonic.

INTRODUCTION TO THE CHORD SCALE THEORY

As mentioned, many elements of traditional harmony can be found in jazz. Theoretical fundamentals, especially parts of functional harmony, have been adapted and developed over time, which resulted in a comprehensive concept of contemporary harmony and provides a new access to the examination of chords, harmonic progressions and their functional relationship: *The Chord Scale Theory.*

In tonal harmony, chords are built in thirds. (The term "tonal harmony" usually refers to the music composed between 1650 and 1900.) While traditional practice uses triads primarily, contemporary harmony refers to seventh chords. The three functional groups are still applicable (tonic, subdominant, dominant).

However, there is a main difference between the chord scale theory and traditional analysis. The latter describes music for theoretical purposes and does not consider the potential possibilities which lie within given harmonic structures. Jazz and related music is an art form, not reproducing one and the same version of a piece over centuries, but deals with improvisation, innovation, and arrangements. The chord scale theory describes a chord or chord progression with all its potential tonal possibilities. So new musical material can be derived simply by analyzing a piece of music and assigning the correct chord scales.

It might be helpful for classical composers to analyze traditional pieces with the tools of chord scales. It offers a new approach to the understanding and writing of music. Music is no longer an unchangeable relic of the past.

The Chord Scale Theory describes the **interrelation between chords and scales**. They form a functional unity with two different manifestations, each representing the qualities of the other.

Chords form a vertical structure of notes (tertian structure), while scales describe a horizontal one (stepwise order). Extended chord structures (thirteenth chords) contain all notes of the appropriate scale. If this vertical structure is turned into a horizontal line, the chord becomes the corresponding scale and vice versa.

The function of a chord in relation to a tonal center determines its structure plus corresponding scale (= chord scale). The subject of the following chapters is to show how to determine a chord's function and to explain common chord progressions.

For identification of chord scales, modal terminology is used. The tonal material from the example above refers to the key of F major (one flat), starting on the fourth scale degree. The chord symbol is B♭maj7(♯11) and the name of the scale is Lydian. With every new chord the scale changes. Since each chord is analyzed separately, this is also vertical analysis.

Vertical and horizontal analysis:

Horizontal: All chords contain the same tonal material, the C major scale. (This works only with diatonic progressions.)

Vertical: Each chord, depending on its function, has its own scale: Cmaj7 = Ionian, A–7 = Aeolian, D–7 = Dorian, G7 = Mixolydian.

Both results seem to be similar in terms of tonal material, but only the second method considers the quality of each scale degree in relationship to the chord.

If the chord changes contain non-diatonic tones, vertical analysis is necessary. The second chord of this example shows a C♯, although the progression is definitely in the key of C major. The tonal material for this chord scale is derived by altering the note C to C♯.

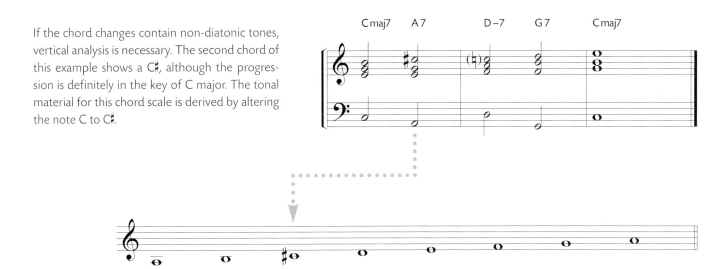

Chord scales have three qualities:

1. **Chord Tones:** The basic chord structures are seventh chords.

2. **Tensions:** Additional tones which create special sound colors and tension.

3. **Avoid Notes:** Tones of a chord scale, which sound very dissonant and therefore are avoided harmonically.

For the description and **analysis** of harmonic progressions Roman numerals and some additional symbols provide the tools of the Chord Scale Theory. They form a symbolic language, which allows one to identify the chords' function, their relationship to a given key, and their relationship to each other.

The categories of chords used in the chord scale theory are:

- Primary Chords (Diatonic Chords)
- Secondary Dominants and Related II Chords
- Sequential Dominants
- Sequential Substitute Dominants
- Modal Interchange Chords (with Subdominant Minor Chords)
- Blues Chords
- Chords with Special Functions
- Non-functional Chords

APPLICATION OF
CONTEMPORARY HARMONY

> ## DIFFERENCES AND SIMILARITIES
> ## TO TRADITIONAL HARMONY

Key Relationships: The traditional definitions are still applicable for *relative* and *parallel* key relationships. Relative keys share the same diatonic; parallel keys share the same tonal center.

Scales: The melodic minor scale is the same descending as ascending (see *Minor Key Harmony*)

Voice Leading: In general, parallel octaves and fifths are not only allowed, but most often required. They hardly occur in traditional tonal music (1650 - 1900). Because of their strong, specific character, parallel motion affects the independence of the individual parts and the balance of a composition. In jazz, chords are heard as functional sounds rather than as a result of independent melodic lines; parallels are typical.

The actual position of a chord's pitches (= voicing) depends on the performer's or arranger's taste and skills. Slash chords (inversions, hybrids and polychords) also contain additional information about voicings. They are most typical of contemporary jazz. (Refer to *Voicing Specific Chord Symbols and Structures.*)

Chord symbols: In contrast to traditional notation, chords built upon various scale degrees are always indicated by capitals or the upper case form of Roman numerals for analysis, no matter if major or minor (refer to *Harmonic Structures*). Additional accidentals raise or lower the natural scale degrees: F♯, ♭III (notice that accidentals precede Roman numerals, while chord symbols precede accidentals). In jazz the readability and understanding of chord symbols and written music in general is most important.

Enharmonic spelling: For the reasons mentioned above, double sharps and double flats are avoided, e.g.,

$$Cx = D, \quad G\flat\flat = F$$

Numbering of scale degrees: Chord scales use numerals, from 1 to 13, for the description of scale degrees. Numbers below in parentheses are usually replaced by their lower representatives. The 9th, 11th and 13th are important indicators of a chord scale. The 7th scale degree of a major scale is maj7 and not 7, which means minor 7th.

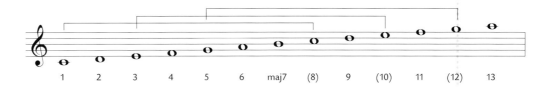

Scale degrees may be altered: minor third = –3; diminished fifth = °5 or ♭5; augmented fifth = +5; minor seventh = 7 (or to make clear –7, or ♭7), diminished seventh = °7. Tensions are preceded by the appropriate accidentals.

Intervals: Like scale degrees, intervals can also be characterized by using Arabian numerals plus accidental, e.g., 13th = major thirteenth, ♯11th = augmented eleventh, ♭9th = minor ninth, 7th = minor seventh.

Depending on context, major and augmented intervals may also be called "raised" or "sharp;" diminished and minor intervals "lowered" or "flat."

Octave registers: The notation of pitch is related to the piano keyboard. The lowest C is designated as C1, therefore the middle C represents C4. (This notation is recommended by the "International Acoustical Society.")

1

Harmonic

Structures

S ome of this immediate information may be so basic to the reader as to appear trivial. Don't skip over it! Some of these concepts may not agree with yours but we must use a common language to converse. Although there are many dialects in our language, this book will use those most familiar. The terms will be those most universally understood. If there are other terms they will be included. However, *any terms which are not understood by the professional working musician will not be used.*

The construction of contemporary chords follows the traditional intervallic relationships of thirds. Triads are foundational. Chords with contents higher than the seventh degree are very common, especially in jazz related contexts. Seventh chords with added 9th, and/or 11th, and/or 13th are normal. In fact the extensions are so common that these pitches are implicitly understood and are not included as part of the chord indicator. The 9th, 11th, and 13th chords will be shown later.

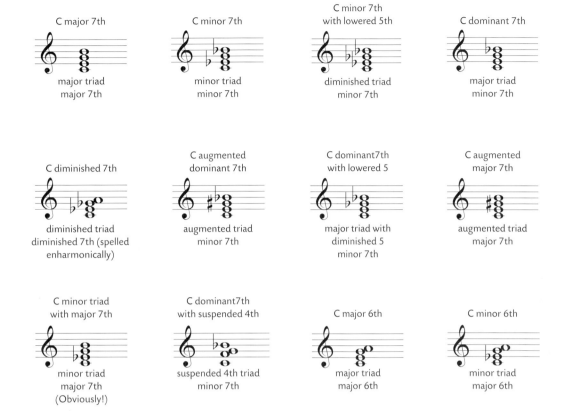

Some observations about a few of these chords:

- The minor 7th with a lowered 5th is not identified as a half diminished chord. This will be explained.
- The 7th of the diminished 7th chord is often notated without double flats.
- The dominant 7th with a suspended 4th does not contain a supporting triad constructed in thirds.
- The suspended 4th is a replacement for the 3rd of the dominant 7th chord.

There are other chord types, but not as common as those above.

CHORD SYMBOLS

Contemporary music symbols are the shorthand of the twentieth century as figured bass was the shorthand of the eighteenth century for notating chords. Chord symbols convey a basic sound, which, at the whim of the performer/writer, may be added to or even simplified. The abbreviation of indicator has progressed slowly and without control. As a result, we have chord symbology that is not universal and subject to much tampering and innovation. Chord symbols are still being developed. Some symbol innovations have fallen by the wayside; some have been accepted. A Berklee colleague has catalogued at least 100 symbols that mean "major seventh chord!" In general, chord symbols should be as universal as possible. Being inventive is great, but if one is not understood, what's the use?

Therefore, some important guide lines for the use of chord symbols:

- Chord symbols are a form of abbreviation and should be as simple as possible for any given situation, regardless of style.

- Experimentation is unnecessary. When in doubt, use written notation.

- Any alterations or additions to a chord should be included in parentheses to separate them from the basic chord sound.

- Some recent innovations in chord symbols are confusing and incorrect. (The most prominent of these will be shown.)

- There is a distinct difference in symbols written in type or by hand. Some graphics do not lend themselves to handwriting done carelessly or fast. For example, a capital M and a lower case m, when written by hand may be confused.

- For chord symbols, ♭ means lowered; ♯ means raised; + means augmented; − means minor.

- Graphics should not be created using letters or numerals. A seven with a slash through it is still a 7, not an abbreviation for "major" 7. (This phenomenon occurs in the United States.)

Chord symbols contain four bits of information always in this order:

1. The root of the chord (capital letters are used).

2. The quality of the supporting triad: major, minor, augmented, diminished. Graphics are often used here (+ means augmented; − means minor; ° means diminished; major is implicitly understood).

3. The highest degree of the structure when built in 3rds above the root: 7th (understood to be minor 7th, or diminished 7th for a diminished 7th chord), 9th, 11th, or 13th.

4. Any alterations or added pitches to the chord. (This is the part of the symbol contained in parentheses and may or may not be necessary.)

Chord symbols for the chords listed on page 21 are:

major 7th: Cmaj7 (or CMaj7) is universally understood and preferred. CMa7 is acceptable. Common symbols include CM7 which can be confused with Cm7 (an alternative for C minor 7) if written by hand and not typeset. CMj7 has the same problem inasmuch as it may appear as Cmi7. The use of C△7 is becoming very popular. It is easy to write and almost universal in meaning but there are some drawbacks; the △ originally meant "triad" and if written with haste may appear as a circle.

minor 7th: C–7 or Cmin7 is universally understood and preferred. Cm7 and Cmi7 are explained above. –7 will be used for the remainder of this text. (Most of us have grown accustomed to the use of a minus sign as meaning minor.)

minor 7th with lowered fifth: C–7(♭5) or Cmin7(♭5) is universally understood and preferred. Here is an instance where the use of parentheses is necessary to show an alteration. The chord symbol indicates a minor 7th chord with an altered 5th. Why not use the traditional ø as a half diminished indicator? Cø (or Cø7) is almost universally recognized but the argument against it is based on the function of the chord as a minor 7th with altered 5th and not a diminished 7th chord with an altered 7th. The unacceptable use of either Cm7(♭5) or Cmi7(♭5) is explained above. For this book –7(♭5) will be used.

dominant 7th: C7 is universally understood and preferred. There are no other legitimate offerings for this symbol.

diminished 7th: Cº7 is universally understood and preferred. Cdim7 is also acceptable.

augmented dominant 7th: C+7 is universally understood and preferred. C7(♯5) and Caug7 are also acceptable.

dominant 7th with lowered fifth: C7(♭5) is universally understood and preferred.

augmented major 7th: C+maj7 is universally understood and preferred. Cmaj7(♯5) and Cmaj7(+5) are also acceptable.

minor triad with major 7th: C–(maj7) and Cmin(maj7) is universally understood. This symbol is indicating two separate qualities in the same location; the supporting triad is minor and the 7th is major. Parentheses are necessary to separate the opposing qualities. –(maj7) will be used for the remainder of this text.

dominant 7th with suspended 4th: C7(sus4) is universally understood and preferred. Do not use C4 or C47 or any other such creature. C11 is also used but is not recommended. It implies a structure in thirds containing root, **3rd**, 5th, minor 7th, 9th, and 11th. The 3rd should not be in a suspended 4th chord.

major 6th: C6 is universally understood and preferred.

minor 6th: C–6 and Cmin6 is universally understood. –6 will be used for the remainder of this text.

Other chord symbols that deserve consideration include triads:

C indicates a major triad; Cmin or C– a minor triad; C+ or Caug an augmented triad; C° or Cdim a diminished triad; C(sus4) a suspended 4th triad. The preferred method of indicating the color tone of the 9th is as an added pitch in parentheses following the symbol: C(add 9); Cmin(add 9); C+(add 9); C°(add 9). The name of the 9th degree may be substituted for the numeral. Hence, the symbol C(add D). The use of C(sus2) is becoming more common in popular/rock styles. Like sus4, sus2 replaces the third (suspension from below) and not the root of the chord, which would be impossible. C(9) or C–(9) is not recommended. These triads are easily confused with 7th chords containing an added 9th.

Inversions, hybrid structures, polychords, and other voicing-specific chord symbols will be examined later. The following summary uses randomly chosen roots:

CHORD SYMBOL SUMMARY

D♭maj7	major 7
B–7	minor 7
G♯–7(♭5)	minor 7, flat 5
G7	dominant 7
B♭°7	diminished 7
A+7	augmented dominant 7
B♭7(♭5)	dominant 7, flat 5
G♭+maj7	augmented major 7
C♯–(maj7)	minor, major 7
E7(sus4)	sus4
C6	major 6
F–6	minor 6
F♯	major triad
E♭–	minor triad
A♭+	augmented triad
D♯°	diminished triad
A♭(addB♭)	major triad, add 9

SYMBOLS FOR ANALYSIS

For analysis purposes – contrary to traditional practice – only upper case Roman numerals are used to avoid misunderstandings like V for v (especially when handwritten). The indicators and additions (min, 7,...) are the same used for chord symbols. The advantage of Roman numerals is that it shows both the quality of the chord and its relationship to a diatonic context, it is not dependent on a specific key.

To review: the following chord symbol defines the notes of the 7th chord:

And, at the same time *implies* the upper extensions of the chord (9th, 11th, 13th):

Not all seven pitches are harmonically stable, but they are *melodically available*:

When arranged as a scale, the harmonic and melodic pitches are a *chord scale*. The chord scale defines basic harmonic and limited melodic activity (when compared to the chromatic scale) for a given chord symbol.

The individual components of a chord scale are:

1. CHORD TONES,

2. available TENSION(S),

3. harmonically AVOIDED NOTE(S).

Chord Tones are self explanatory.

Tensions are the upper extension of the 7th chord that color the chord and *do not alter the intended sound*.

The **Avoid Note**, if used harmonically, will interfere with, or destabilize the chord sound and is therefore *avoided* harmonically.

Avoid notes are nonchord tones which are *a half step above* a chord tone. They are marked as black notes. If the avoid note is used harmonically, it will destabilize the chord. There are a few situations where, through centuries of usage and cultural conditioning, we have grown accustomed to accepting this occurrence. These exceptions only occur on the Dorian chord scale and on dominant 7th chords (because of their inherent instability).

All the notes of the scale are available melodically

When a chord scale is examined, the notes will have the same intervallic relationship as one of the common modal scales. The modal name is used regardless of the compositional context.

The **Ionian chord scale** contains:

- the chord tones of a major 7th chord (1, 3, 5, maj7), and

- available tensions 9 and 13 (scale degrees 2 and 6), and

- an avoided 4th degree (11th).

Cmaj7 = C Ionian

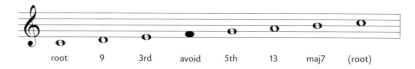

Context will determine the choice of pitches. The F natural is obviously a pitch from the key of C major. In the key of G major, the note would be F sharp and be an available tension in a **Lydian chord scale**:

Cmaj7 = C Lydian

As with chord symbols, ♭ means "lowered", ♯ means "raised."

The chord scales used for major 7th and major 6th chords are the above mentioned Ionian and Lydian scales. Major 6 and minor 6 chords are used as alternatives for the maj7 and min(maj)7 chords especially if the melody pitch is the root of a chord containing maj7. The root should represent an avoid note inasmuch as it is a half step above the major 7th. The melody can not be avoided. The alternative 6th chord is used to compensate for this dilemma.

The chord scales used for –7th chords are:

C–7 = C Dorian

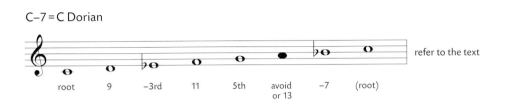

refer to the text

C–7 = C Aeolian

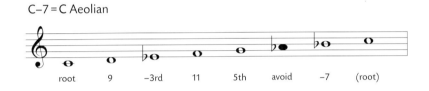

C–7 = C Phrygian

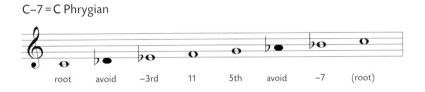

The 6th degree of the Dorian scale is an acceptable whole step above the 5th, *but* it is still avoided. All other –7 chord scales avoid the 6th degree. In the Dorian chord scale, major 6th along with the minor 3rd of the chord creates a tritone which is the basis for dominant sound and function. This exception to avoid notes is slowly changing, especially in jazz situations where 13 occurs as a melody pitch. More and more we will find a Dorian chord scale being used with 13 as an available tension. For now it will be considered an avoid note. Although avoid notes do not occur harmonically, their inclusion melodically is what defines a specific function for a chord. Avoid notes are the pitches from which each chord derives its characteristic sound.

The chord scale used for the –7(♭5) chord is *Locrian:*

C–7(♭5) = Locrian

root   avoid   –3rd   11   ♭5th   ♭13   –7   (root)

The chord scales for dominant 7th chords are too numerous to mention at this point. They will be introduced gradually. The two most common **dominant 7th chord scales** are *Mixolydian and Lydian ♭7*:

C7 = C Mixolydian

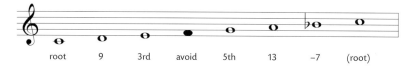

root   9   3rd   avoid   5th   13   –7   (root)

C7 = C Lydian ♭7

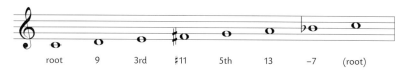

root   9   3rd   ♯11   5th   13   –7   (root)

The Lydian ♭7 scale is nondiatonic to any key. (Nondiatonic means "not belonging to a controlling tonal center." "Nondiatonic" will also be used when referring to a chord's function.) Also of importance is the fact that Lydian ♭7 has *not* been identified as a Mixolydian ♯11. There is a significant reason for this distinction, that will eventually be examined in detail.

The **chord scale** used for the **+7th** and the **7(♭5)** chord is *whole-tone*. The 7(♭5) is most often a wrong spelling for dominant 7(♯11); the real 7(♭5) is rare.

C+7 and C7(♭5) = whole-tone

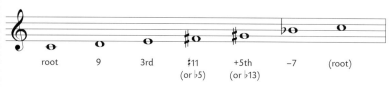

root   9   3rd   ♯11   +5th   –7   (root)
                       (or ♭5)   (or ♭13)

The **chord scale** used for a dominant **7th (sus4)** is a Mixolydian chord scale but the *avoid note is the 3rd*:

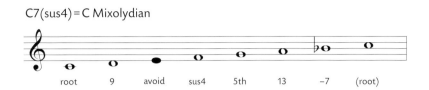

C7(sus4) = C Mixolydian

| root | 9 | avoid | sus4 | 5th | 13 | −7 | (root) |

The chord scales used for °**7th chords** are also numerous. Each will be examined individually. For now, a common scale associated with the °7th chord is:

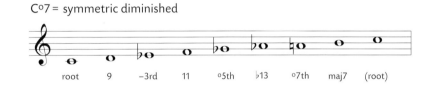

C°7 = symmetric diminished

| root | 9 | −3rd | 11 | °5th | ♭13 | °7th | maj7 | (root) |

This last scale contains eight pitches. This situation creates an unusual numbering pattern. In this case, the available tensions include major 7 which is usually considered a chord tone. This scale will be examined later.

CHORD SCALE SUMMARY

Ionian for maj7 and maj6 chords

Dorian, Phrygian, Aeolian for −7 chords

Lydian for maj7 and maj6 chords

Mixolydian for dominant 7 and dominant 7(sus4) chords

Locrian for −7(♭5) chords

Lydian ♭7 for dominant 7 chords

whole-tone for +7 and 7(♭5) chords

symmetric diminished for °7 chords

AVOID NOTE SUMMARY

Ionian: avoid 11 (= 4)

Dorian: avoid 13 (= 6)

Phrygian: avoid ♭9 and ♭13 (= ♭2 and ♭6)

Mixolydian: avoid 11 (= 4) – avoid 3 for (sus4)

Aeolian: avoid ♭13 (= ♭6)

Locrian: avoid ♭9 (= ♭2)

Lydian, Lydian ♭7, whole-tone and symmetric diminished have no avoid notes

2

Diatonic

Harmony

We can now begin to look at specific tonal relationships within chord progressions. Every chord has a function or tonal responsibility. When we hear a chord progression we match each chord sound to a function. How is the chord working to make the music progress forward? Our subconscious instantly justifies the chord's function as it passes our mind's ear even if it is a chord one had previously not expected to hear. Perception of function occurs in a split second. The more experienced the listener, the better the understanding of how each event relates to the total picture. (This concept of functional harmony can be traced back to Hugo Riemann who taught at the University of Leipzig.) The basis for functional harmony is *sound*, not labeling. There are three basic sound groups in diatonic harmony:

- tonic,
- subdominant,
- dominant.

The traditional names for the diatonic chords are based on root location within the key. We are only concerned with the three functional sounds of tonic, sub-dominant, and dominant:

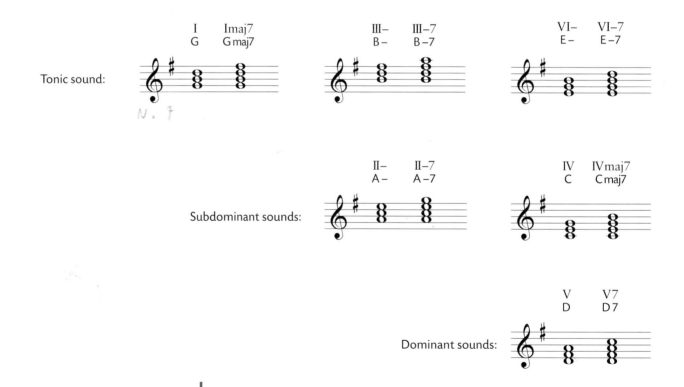

The symbols of analysis are not the same as those used for traditional triadic analysis. The Roman numerals are all *upper case* because the chord quality of major or minor is included in the chord symbol. A II–7 chord will be the same as a ii–7 chord.

- The characteristic pitch of the major key is the *unstable 4th scale degree.*

- The tonic sounds of the key are chords *without* the unstable characteristic pitch as a chord tone.

- The subdominant chords contain, as a chord tone, the unstable character pitch separate from the *very unstable diatonic tritone* (scale degrees 4 and 7).

- The dominant 7th chord *contains* the character pitch as a component of the *diatonic tritone*.

- The VII–7(♭5) chord is missing from the diatonic listing. This chord will continually appear as an ambiguous entity. Although the VII–7(♭5) contains the character pitch, in contemporary usage it is never (at most – very rarely) a diatonic dominant sound. The VII–7(♭5) contains the diatonic tritone, however, a necessary ingredient for dominant function is the position of the tritone. With few exceptions *the tritone interval must represent the 3rd and the 7th of a chord with dominant function*:

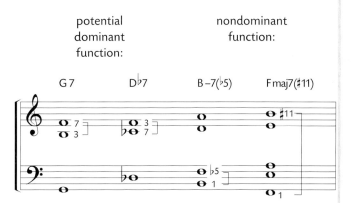

Any chord may follow the tonic chord *because it represents total stability. Any diatonic chord may progress to any other diatonic chord.* The control factor is in the relationship between the roots of the chords and the voice leading between chords.

ROOT MOTION AND PATTERNS

If the diatonic chords in the key of C major are arranged in steps (2nds) and their functional sound is examined, the unfolding of harmonic progression from most stable to least stable can be seen. (For demonstration purposes, the VII–7(♭5) has been awarded a questionable dominant function.):

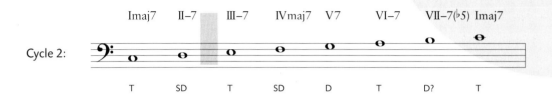

Notice when diatonic chords move in stepwise root motion, there will be movement of unstable nontonic sound to stable tonic sound or unstable to very unstable then to tonic (except when the V7 moves down to IVmaj7). This defines *progression*, with the exception of the *retrogression* of V7 to IVmaj7 (an uncommon chord pattern in jazz contexts except in the blues).

If the chords are arranged in root motion of diatonic 5ths, the same symmetry of function will occur, only here the patterns are unstable – very unstable – stable, except in retrograde:

This root motion of 5ths represents the building up of tension and then its release. Notice the only place in the pattern of motion where the string of perfect 5ths changes is when moving down to the VII–7(♭5). This 5th pattern, when inverted, will create retrogressions except when II–7 moves to VI–7 and IVmaj7 moves to Imaj7.

If the diatonic chords are arranged in root motion of diatonic 3rds, a different symmetric pattern of events occurs. Root motion in 3rds is usually downward:

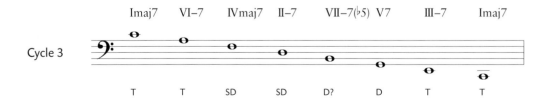

Diatonic root motion in 3rds is the most subtle because chords of the same function are heard next to one another. This only changes roots, not sound. However, there does remain the movement of nontonic to tonic.

- The strongest diatonic root motion is down in 5ths.

- Stepwise diatonic root motion is also strong.

- Diatonic root motion down in 3rds is weaker than the above but is found in progressions.

- The use of diatonic root motion in 4ths creates patterns which are retrograde of the patterns in 5ths. This will tend to create retrogressions of stable tonic chords moving to very unstable sounds. (IVmaj7 to Imaj7 is the primary exception.)

Chord scales determine the function of the chords in the major key. Diatonic chords use diatonic chord scales associated with the displacement of the Ionian scale:

- Ionian · · · · · · · Imaj7

- Dorian · · · · · · II–7

- Phrygian · · · · · III–7

- Lydian · · · · · · · IVmaj7

- Mixolydian · · · V7

- Aeolian · · · · · VI–7

- Locrian · · · · · VII–7(♭5)

V7 to Imaj7 is the strongest diatonic root motion in the key because it represents the most unstable to most stable chords available. An arrow is used to show *dominant resolution down a perfect fifth*. Resolution means movement from the dominant root down a perfect 5th.

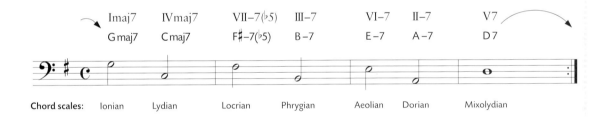

The arrow is *not* used if the root motion is not down a perfect 5th. In the cases where the V7 chord moves to either the III–7 or the VI–7, *diatonic deceptive resolution* occurs (refer to *Cadences*). We are so used to hearing this deceptive resolution that it does not sound very deceptive at all. Roman numerals (without an arrow) will indicate that the dominant is moving to a tonic other than Imaj7. In jazz, nondiatonic deceptive resolutions are common; they are part of the following chapters. The significance of using the arrow to show dominant resolution will become apparent when looking at cadences that are nondiatonic.

CADENCES

The cadence is the most important harmonic formula in music. It represents or confirms a tonal center and therefore appears mostly at the end of a musical section. In general the chords of a cadence form a harmonic goal or are heading for one. All types of traditional cadences also apply to jazz, though some are more important than others. The most important progression, as mentioned before, is V7 going to I, known as **authentic cadence** or **authentic resolution**:

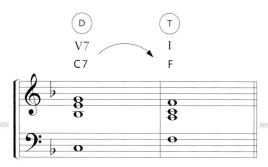

The **plagal cadence** or **plagal resolution** is most often found in Blues (refer to chapter *Blues*), but may be also found in popular songs like "Yesterday" by the Beatles.

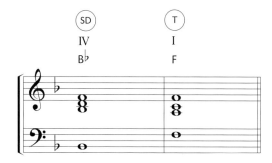

Notice that no arrow is used.

A cadence which rests temporarily to a dominant chord on a stress point is a *half cadence*. Harmonic rhythm is an important factor; it will be discussed (*Harmonic Rhythm* and *Sequential Dominants*). Half cadences are very unstable because of the dominant's placement.

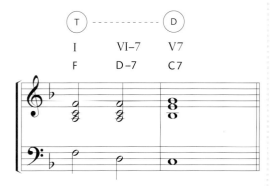

A special type of half cadence is the traditionally labeled **Phrygian half cadence**, where the V7 is preceded by ♭VImaj7 or ♭VI6 (= 1st inversion of IV−7). Both imply subdominant sound (refer to *Minor Key Harmony* and *Modal Interchange*). Antonio Carlos Jobim's tune "Chega De Saudade" contains a Phrygian half cadence:

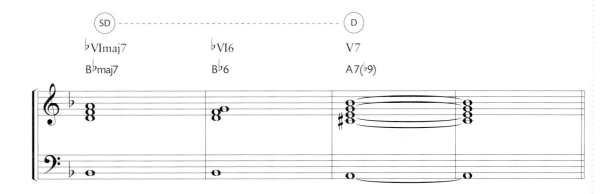

A **deceptive resolution** occurs when the resolution of a V chord is not the expected I chord. While in traditional music only diatonic deceptive cadences appear (V going to VI− or III−; Arnold Schönberg also considered retrogression to the IV chord deceptive), contemporary music also applies different nondiatonic deceptive progressions. For now only the diatonic deceptive cadences are shown:

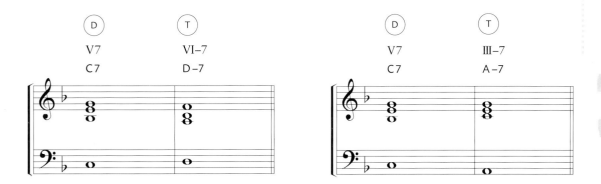

Notice that no arrow is used, because the root motion is not down a perfect 5th.

The following cadences show deceptive resolution to ♭VI, which is natural to minor key, but also available in major (refer to *Minor Key Harmony*, *Modal Interchange*).

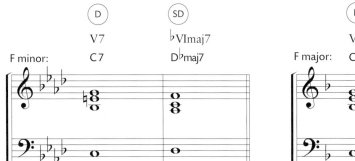

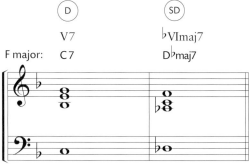

THE II V I CADENCE

The resolution V to I is the basis of tonal music. But which chord precedes the dominant? Most often a subdominant chord, which appears as a IV or II chord. If one considers the II–7 chord a subdominant sound, and the strongest root motion is descending perfect fifths, one can appreciate why most contemporary music styles contain the typical cadence progression II–7 V7 Imaj7. When these chords are arranged in this order, the functional sounds of the key occur in a logical sequence. Because of this strong root relationship, the II–7 V7 progression deserves a special indicator. The bracket beneath the II–7 and V7 chords shows this relationship. Again, the significance of the bracket will become obvious where nondiatonic cadences occur:

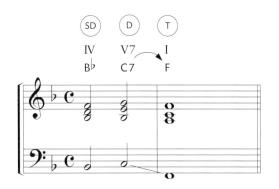

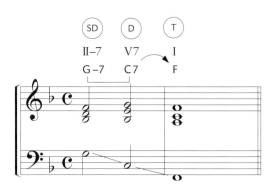

└────┘ *indicates a –7 moving down a perfect 5th to a dominant 7;*

⌒→ *indicates a dominant 7th or dominant 7th(sus4) resolution down a perfect 5th to the root of a target chord:*

⌒→ *becomes:*   G–7   C7   F root
└────┘   └────┘

Although the IV V I chord progression is the most popular cadence in classical music, a number of examples with a II V I cadence can be found in the Baroque and Romantic period. The following example is an excerpt of J. S. Bach's Prelude in C from the "Well-Tempered Clavier." It contains seventh chords like a II V jazz progression:

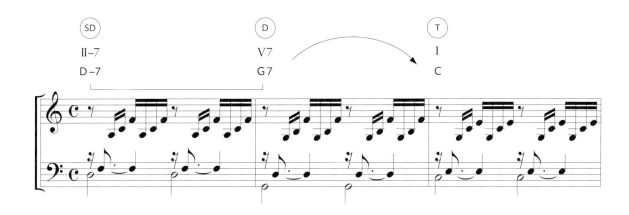

The II V I cadence in minor key will be discussed in more detail (refer to *Related II–7 Chords* and *Minor Key Harmony*). The same analysis symbols apply:

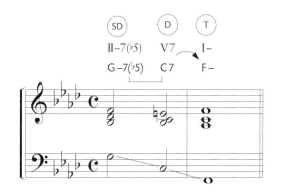

In traditional music the II V I cadence in a minor key rarely appears, because the II chord contains a lowered 5th which gives an unstable diminished triad. This chord actually functions as a minor triad with an altered 5th. For this reason in jazz the II–7(♭5) of a II V cadence is not considered a half diminished chord, because it is an altered minor 7th chord and not an altered diminished 7th chord. Here is an example of a II–7(♭5) found in the music of the 18th century:

J. S. Bach, BWV 343

This is also a good example for showing the relationship between the II and IV chord (subdominant).

In jazz the II V I cadence has become the most important chord progression. The strong II V relationship developed as an independent unit with no need to resolve to the tonic, although the tendency still exists. It can appear unresolved several times in a row as Duke Ellington's "Satin Doll" shows:

SUS4 CHORDS

The V7(sus4) chord is a common variation of a diatonic chord. Unlike the other diatonic structures, the function of V7(sus4) is dependent on context. V7(sus4) contains half of the diatonic tritone (scale degree 4), however, it is built on the *dominant root*. V7(sus4) may be heard as either a dominant or subdominant sound:

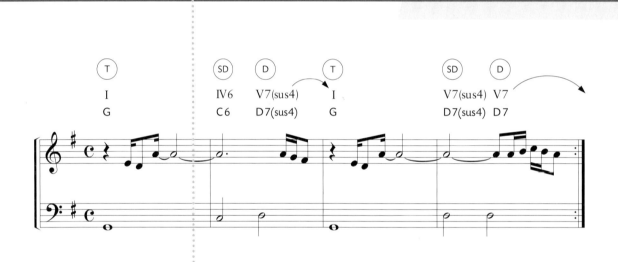

If the V7(sus4) occurs where the normal V7 would be, it is functioning as a dominant; if it occurs where a subdominant chord would be, it is functioning subdominant. In most cases this depends on harmonic rhythm. *Strong stress* – subdominant, *weaker stress* – dominant.

If the V7(sus4) chord has a subdominant function, the chord symbol is often written as either IVmaj7 or II–7 over the root of the V chord. *Hybrids* such as these will be discussed in greater detail.

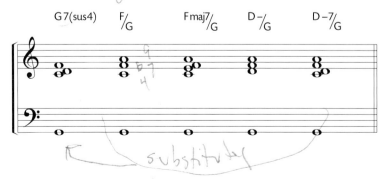

The diagonal slash in the hybrid chord symbols separates the upper structure from the root. This method of symbology, although not universal, is generally understood. A more universal chord symbol is Fmaj7 (G bass).

By substituting other chords with the same functional sound, it is possible to *reharmonize* an existing progression. The end result will be a new chord progression which sounds similar to the original. What follows is a reharmonization of the example from the previous page:

Here are some observations about this simple reharmonization technique:

- The melody remains the same.
- The root motion has changed but the functional sounds have not.
- The melody and reharmonization choices are compatible with the chosen chord scales.
- The original resolutions of the two dominant chords are no longer down a perfect 5th.
- The harmonic rhythm has changed.

DIATONIC TUNES FOR ANALYSIS

"In a Mountain Greenery"

"My Romance" (first section)

"Killing Me Softly" (most of it)

"Mack The Knife"

3

Dominant Chords and
Diatonic Function

SECONDARY DOMINANTS

The strength of dominant resolution lies in root motion *down a perfect 5th*. The primary dominant of the key is the V7 chord:

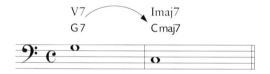

A dominant chord can resolve to any quality of chord. Resolution to a °7th or a
−7(♭5) ("Stella by Starlight") is uncommon. The only requirement for resolution
of a dominant chord is root motion down a perfect 5th:

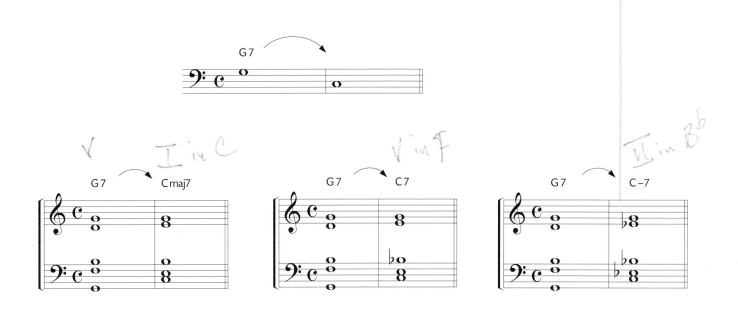

The *primary dominant's* resolution is down a perfect 5th to Imaj7. A *secondary
dominant's* resolution is down a perfect 5th to one of the diatonic chords *other
than Imaj7 or VII−7(♭5)*. (Here again the VII−7(♭5) chord is relegated to a different status.):

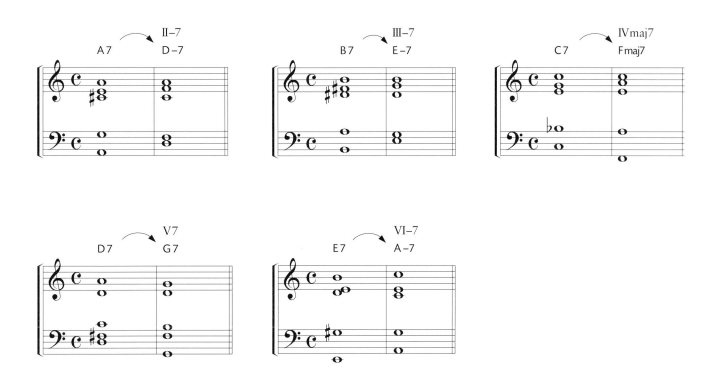

The arrow is used to show resolution down a perfect 5th. Some analysis systems use I7, II7, III7, and so forth, to analyze these secondary dominants. The problem with this method is that it only indicates the chord's position in the key and quality; it does not say how the chord is functioning. Function is all important. The analysis used will indicate that the secondary dominant chord is dominant (V7) of a diatonic chord (II, III, IV, V, VI). To abbreviate this, a slash is used to mean "of." V7/II means V7 *of* II. The quality of the target chord is not necessary. This same analysis is usable, and will eventually be needed, for the primary dominant:

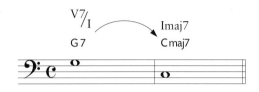

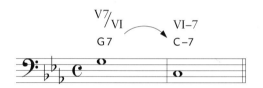

Secondary dominants possess common traits:

- They have at least one nondiatonic chord tone.

- They resolve to a diatonic chord and therefore have a *diatonically related* function.

- The roots are diatonic. (Note that a perfect 5th above VII–7(♭5) is not diatonic.)

The chord scales for secondary dominants reflect these common characteristics: *chord tones and diatonic non-chord tones*:

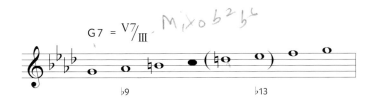

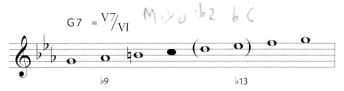

After much experience, with many tunes, in many styles, it becomes apparent that of all the chord qualities, dominant 7th chords create analytical problems. They are the most unstable chords but have the greatest potential for deception. It is impossible to hear a song for the first time and know what *will* happen; we can only hear what is *expected* to happen based on previous experience. There cannot be deceptive motion if a dominant 7th chord scale *tells* the listener that the deception will occur.

The available tensions and the avoid notes for the secondary dominants tell the listener to expect the diatonic target chord. Here are two more exceptions to the avoid note criteria.

- ♭9 *is available.* ♭9 has long been used to help indicate to the listener an expectation of resolution to a chord containing a perfect 5th. If ♭9 is available, ♯9 is also available. ♯9 does not create an avoid note circumstance. These scales will contain 8 different pitches.

- ♭13 *is available.* ♭13 reflects the sound of the expected resolution to a minor chord. (It is the −3rd of the target.) However, there is one caveat. ♭13 sounds like an augmented 5th. If both it and natural 5 are harmonically used, the listener will be confused as to the position of 5. Both are available, but not together; one is *conditional* to the use of the other. The conditional pitches above are in parentheses.

The only true avoid note in the secondary dominant chord scales is the 4th degree (11). The 4th degree represents the root of the expected target chord and is the note harmonically avoided in all Mixolydian scales. *All chords using Mixolydian scales are expected to resolve down a perfect 5th*, hence, these scales are all identified as Mixolydian or Mixolydian with the appropriate alterations to 9 and/or 13:

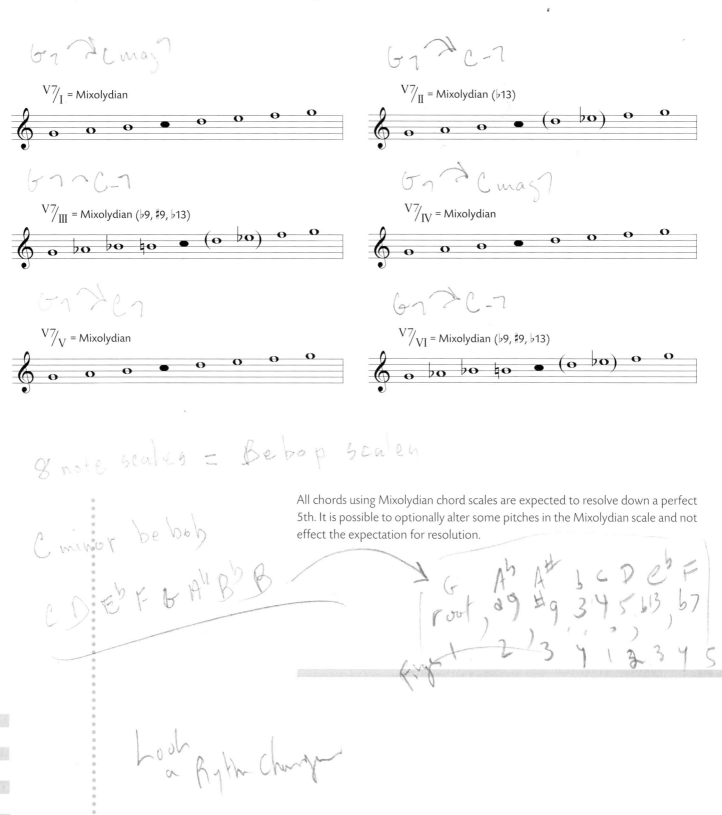

All chords using Mixolydian chord scales are expected to resolve down a perfect 5th. It is possible to optionally alter some pitches in the Mixolydian scale and not effect the expectation for resolution.

The 9th, 5th, and/or the 13th may be altered to ♭9 and ♯9, ♭5, and/or ♭13. *Altered notes should not be changed to unaltered* as this action would change the resolution expectation:

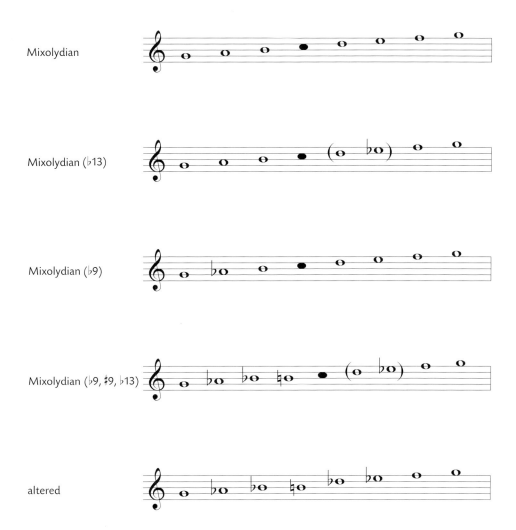

The last scale in the above listing has no avoid notes so it appears as though it is not a form of Mixolydian. Its function remains the same as that of Mixolydian. The altered scale is also know as **diminished/whole-tone**. Other chord scales that function the same as Mixolydian, but do not contain an avoid note, are the whole-tone scale and the symmetric dominant scale. The symmetric dominant chord scale will be discussed at length. The **whole-tone scale** is used for augmented 7th chords:

Notice should be taken that, with the exceptions involving °7th chords, in the world of chord scales *there will be found no situations where the same numbered pitch will appear unaltered as well as altered*. For example, a Mixolydian scale containing ♮5 and ♭5.

PRIMARY AND SECONDARY DOMINANT CHORD SCALES

Summary

V7/I   ···Mixolydian – Mixolydian with alterations – altered – whole-tone

V7/II   ···Mixolydian (♭13) – Mixolydian (♭9, ♯9, ♭13) – altered – whole-tone

V7/III ··Mixolydian (♭9, ♯9, ♭13) – altered – whole-tone

V7/IV   ··Mixolydian – Mixolydian with alterations – altered – whole-tone

V7/V   ··Mixolydian – Mixolydian with alterations – altered – whole-tone

V7/VI   ··Mixolydian (♭9, ♯9, ♭13) – altered – whole-tone

The following chord progression will demonstrate another important characteristic of secondary dominant chords. The primary and secondary dominants resolve *from weak* stress points *to stronger* stress points. If a dominant chord does not meet this criteria, it will have problems being heard functionally as a secondary dominant. In order to understand this distinction it will be necessary to investigate harmonic rhythm:

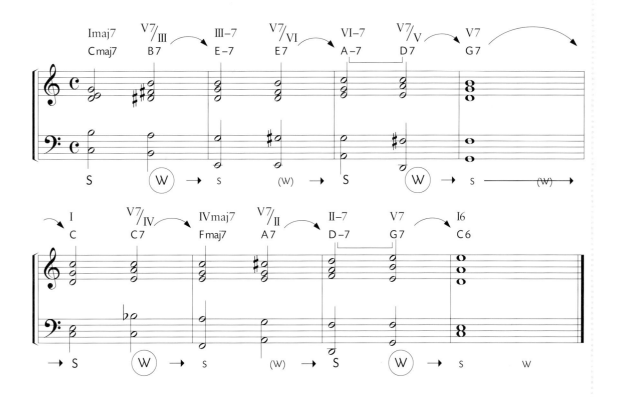

In the above example the A–7 D7 has been analyzed with a bracket. This is an example of a *dual function*. The A–7 is the diatonic VI–7 chord and also the related II–7 of D7. A–7 D7 can always be heard as a II–7 V7, but in this key it is not the diatonic II–7 V7. The dual analysis allows for an option of chord scale choices; either the diatonic chord scale for VI–7 or a Dorian (II–7) chord scale. This is artistic judgement on the part of the composer, arranger, or player.

When V7/IV *resolves* to IVmaj7, the nondiatonic pitch of this secondary dominant is retained by the listener (the C7 to Fmaj7 above) and, *the chord scale for the IVmaj7 is Ionian*. This is the only maj7 chord with this chord scale choice.

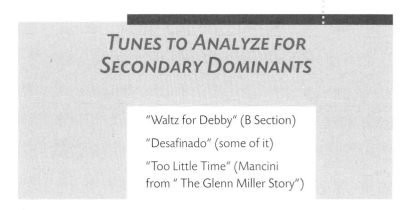

TUNES TO ANALYZE FOR SECONDARY DOMINANTS

"Waltz for Debby" (B Section)

"Desafinado" (some of it)

"Too Little Time" (Mancini from " The Glenn Miller Story")

HARMONIC RHYTHM

Harmonic rhythm is the rate of harmonic change. In common time the typical rhythms are 2, 4 and 8 beats per chord:

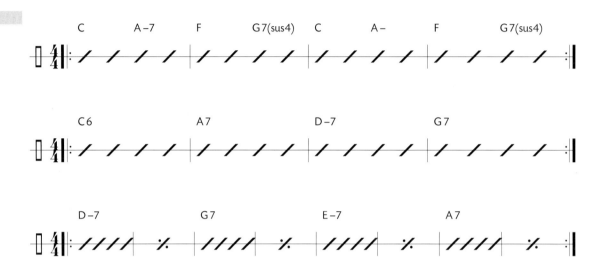

In triple meters the common rhythms are 3 and 6 beats per chord:

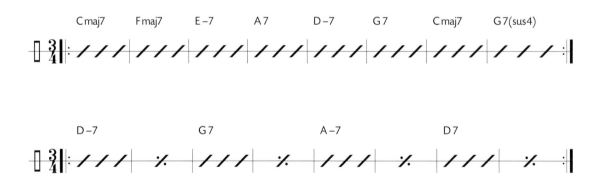

In any grouping of rhythmic pulsations, we tend to hear multiples of four. The first pulse is the strongest; the third is not so strong; the second is weaker; the fourth is the weakest:

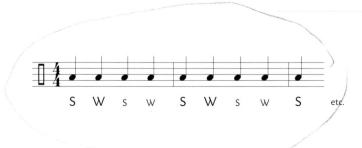

This stress pattern can be demonstrated for any harmonic rhythm:

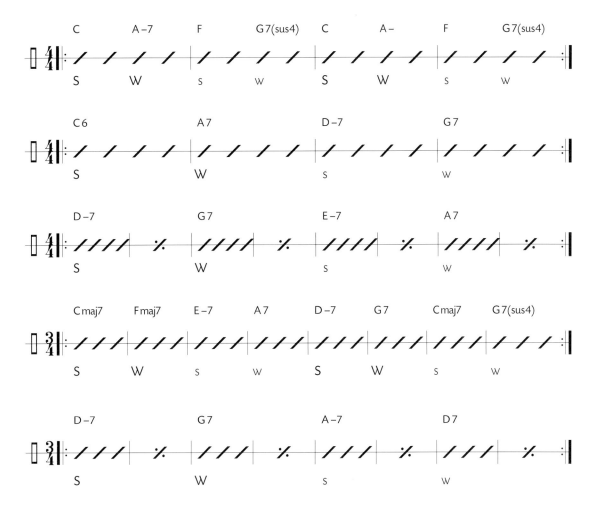

Harmonic cadences, with few exceptions, are found moving from a weak beat to a stronger beat. The V7 chord typically moves to a tonic chord from weak to strong:

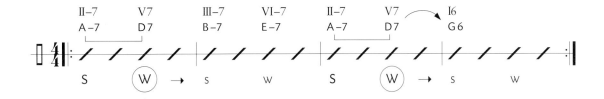

This weak to strong harmonic flow is also typical of secondary dominant resolution. Observe the progression from page 47. The dominant chords are on a weaker stress than the chord of resolution. Strength of stress is always relative. Notice the G7 in measure 4 is on a strong beat that is weaker than the beat to which it resolves:

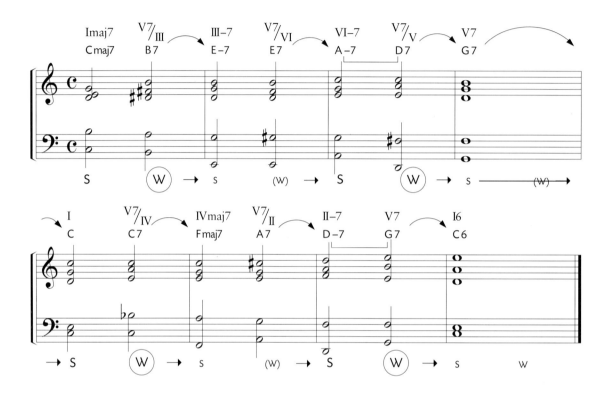

In the real musical world harmonic rhythms will not usually be as evenly spaced as these examples. Overlapping patterns are common; for example, where the 3rd pulse beat becomes the 1st pulse beat of the next pattern as in "The Girl From Ipanema," or, patterns superimposed within larger patterns as in "Sophisticated Lady." Search for interesting harmonic rhythms for their contribution to good compositions is invaluable.

Recall, the characteristics of secondary dominants are:

- They are nondiatonic structures.

- They function diatonically.

- The roots are diatonic.

- They appear on weaker stress points than their chord of resolution.

- There is an expectation for resolution to a diatonic target chord.

Any variation to these criteria may result in a *sequential dominant* (also known as *extended dominant*). Sequential dominants are nondiatonic dominant chords that resolve to other nondiatonic chords such as another sequential dominant or the related II–7 of a sequential dominant. There is an expectation for sequential dominants to eventually return to the diatonic. *Secondary dominants are the source for the sequential dominants.* If the primary and secondary dominants are linked into the cycle of 5ths, the progression would appear as a sequential dominant chord progression:

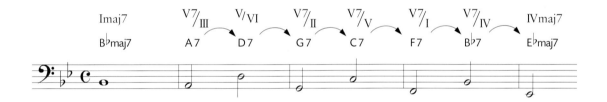

However, these chords are no longer dominant of a diatonic chord; each is dominant of a target dominant chord. Their function is nondiatonic. Compare the characteristics of secondary dominants with

the characteristics of sequential dominants:

- They are nondiatonic structures. (Except V7, if it is in the series, as above.)

- They *do not* function diatonically.

- The roots are diatonic.

- The chord scales *do not* have a diatonic orientation.

- They appear on weak or *strong* stress points.

- There is an expectation for resolution to *another sequential dominant*

The sequential dominant progression above is a little extreme, but examples of it do exist ("Waltz for Debby" by Bill Evans). The most typical of sequential dominant progressions are those which culminate with the V7 chord resolving to Imaj7:

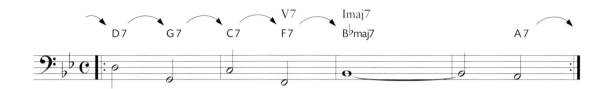

From a theoretical point of view, the F7 is V7 of I; the C7 is V7 of V7 of I; the G7 is V7 of V7 of V7 of I; the D7 is V7 of V7 of V7 of V7 of I; and finally the A7 is:

Quite impractical!

$$V7/_{V7/_{V7/_{V7/_{V7/_{I}}}}}$$

Sequential dominants are expected to resolve to another sequential dominant. Each dominant will sound functionally like a *dominant of a dominant* — V7/V. But to call each a V7/V would be inaccurate because in this key V7/V is C7. Here is a logical place where the use of only an arrow will indicate each resolution.

There are two different ways a sequential dominant series will start. Because all sequential dominants have the same chord sound as secondary dominants, the first chord of a sequence or pattern may represent a secondary dominant resolving deceptively:

Sequential dominant motion will end with a resolution to a diatonic chord.

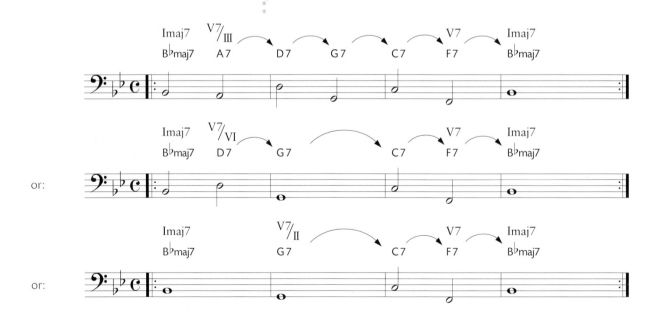

or:

or:

There remains a problem with the above analyses. The first chord in each series is analyzed as a secondary dominant that resolves, but the resolution chord is not the expected diatonic structure.

Parentheses are an analysis symbol that are used to show this deceptive resolution that result in a change of function for the secondary dominant.

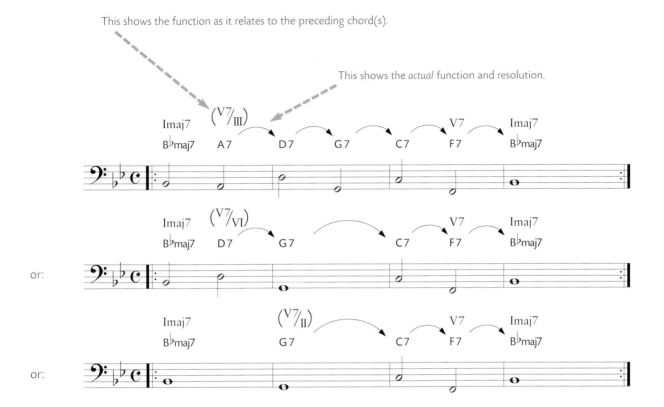

*Parenthetical analysis always shows a **change of function** for a chord.*

The other way a sequential dominant series begins relates to harmonic rhythm and the fact that secondary dominants appear at weaker stress points than their chord of resolution. In the previous examples, the first chord of the series has been ultimately analyzed as a secondary dominant resolving deceptively. But what if the chord was the first chord of the song? Its stress location would be the strongest possible. Strong stress location is not a typical characteristic of secondary dominants. Any dominant heard in this location will be a sequential dominant and analyzed using an arrow for justification. The typical location for this occurrence is at the beginning of a phrase. Here an analysis showing the dominant chord's position in the key will be used because there is no key orientation. (D7 below is (III7), *not* V7/VI.)

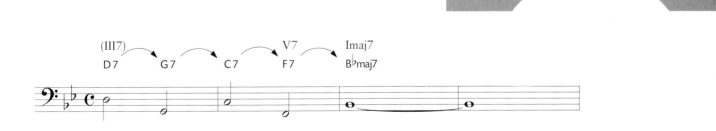

If one studies all this confusing criteria for sequential dominants closely it will be seen that it is possible for a sequential dominant progression to be only one chord that is on a strong stress and resolves to a diatonic chord – starting criterion met – ending criterion met. Unusual, but it does occur. The parentheses are used to show that this, and any sequential dominant, *can* change function and resolve diatonically as a secondary dominant (as demonstrated in the beginning of Jobim's "Quiet Nights" and below):

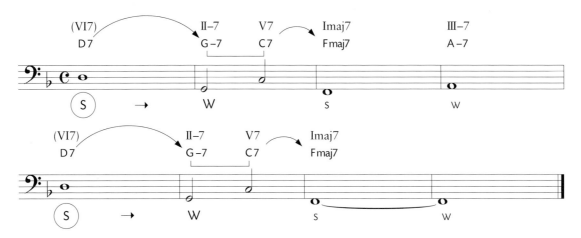

Every sequential dominant in a series will be heard as a dominant of a dominant – V7/V. *The chord scale will be the same as a V7/V – Mixolydian, whether it is diatonic or not:*

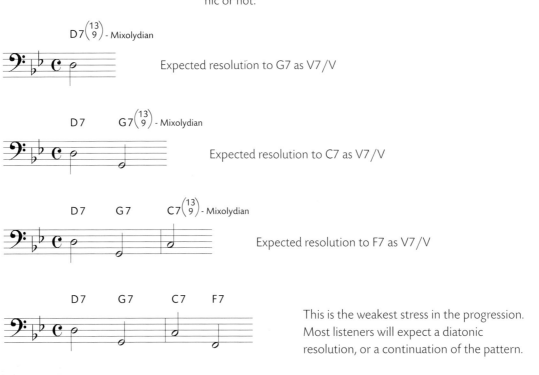

D7($^{13}_{9}$) - Mixolydian

Expected resolution to G7 as V7/V

D7   G7($^{13}_{9}$) - Mixolydian

Expected resolution to C7 as V7/V

D7   G7   C7($^{13}_{9}$) - Mixolydian

Expected resolution to F7 as V7/V

D7   G7   C7   F7

This is the weakest stress in the progression. Most listeners will expect a diatonic resolution, or a continuation of the pattern.

D7   G7   C7   F7   B♭maj7

Chords are first analyzed for their *sound*:

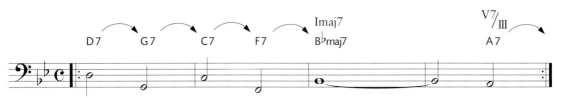

Any *change of function* is parenthesized:

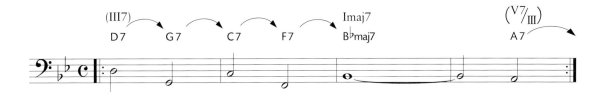

Actual resolution for the deceptive resolution(s) added:

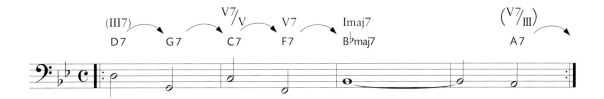

The chord scale for *any* chord that moves deceptively is the chord scale based on the parenthetical analysis. That is the chord's *functional sound*. The A7 above would, as V7/III, use a Mixolydian (♭9, ♯9, ♭13); The D7, as (III7), a sequential dominant, would use Mixolydian!

Some experienced listeners are able to hear through sequential dominant progressions and perceive the V7/V chord not as a sequential dominant but as a secondary dominant of V7, as in the last analysis. In either case, the chord scale for the C7 is Mixolydian. Also, some less experienced listeners may not hear the F7 as the primary dominant but as a part of the sequential dominant chain as in the second to last analysis. The chord scale for F7 is Mixolydian. Both of the last examples have the appropriate analysis.

The preceding information regarding sequential dominants is not etched in stone. There are many ambiguities involved, especially when harmonic rhythm is involved. The tune "All of Me" contains a dominant chord that is on a strong stress and resolves to a weaker stress. *It is not a sequential dominant but a secondary dominant*.

The melody, or chord scale choice, or style, or composer's intention are potential contributing factors to the recognition of sequential dominant chords. The most important consideration is *sound*. If it sounds like a secondary dominant, it is a secondary dominant; if it sounds like a sequential dominant, it is a sequential dominant.

TUNES TO ANALYZE FOR SEQUENTIAL DOMINANTS

"I Got Rhythm" (B section)

"Waltz for Debby" (A section)

"All of Me"

"Quiet Nights" (some of it)

SEQUENTIAL DOMINANTS AND CLASSICAL MUSIC

In classical harmony the term Consecutive Dominants (moving in a cycle of fifths) is more common than Sequential Dominants. W. A. Mozart, among others, used the diatonic instability of sequential dominants to enhance the dramatic effect of a musical situation. Through the increased significance of chromaticism in the 19th century, Sequential Dominants became a common musical device. The most popular example is "Romeo and Juliet" by P. I. Tschaikovsky:

Observe the chord tensions used. Each dominant chord contains at least ♭9 (in the melody or chords) to increase the effect of the dominant sound. This sequence ends with a II–7(♭5) V7(♭9) I cadence (the primary dominant V7 also contains a ♭9, although going to I major). It sounds like a jazz chord progression, although this piece was composed decades before jazz was "invented."

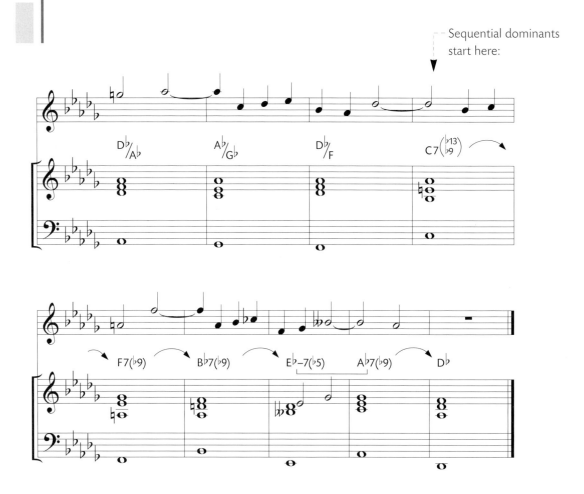

A closer examination of the voice leading of sequential dominants in classical music shows some interesting modifications. While the leading tone of a dominant chord usually resolves up to the root of a diatonic chord, it slides down a half step to the seventh of the next dominant, if a sequence of dominant chords occurs. The 3rd becomes the 7th of the next chord and vice versa. In jazz these notes are called *guide tones*, a series of guide tones is a *guide tone line*.

The instability of a dominant chord is attributed to the tritone. In order for the chord to have a dominant sound, the tritone *must represent the 3rd and 7th of the chord:*

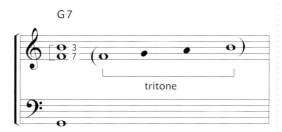

If the tritone is inverted, the enharmonic spelling of the 3rd and 7th can be heard exchanging positions resulting in a different dominant chord root that contains the same tritone:

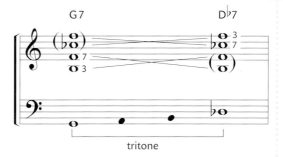

These are *substitute dominant* chords. They are also known as *tritone substitute* chords because they share common tritones and their roots are a tritone apart. In C major, G7 is the primary dominant and Db7 is its substitute dominant. G7 is V7 and Db7 will be analyzed as subV7. This analysis means *substitute for V7.*

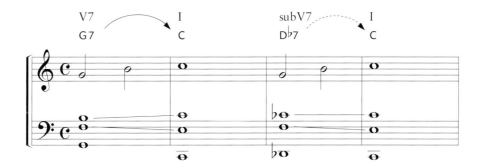

The justification for dominant resolution *down a perfect 5th is a solid arrow*; the resolution of subV7 will be down a half step and indicated with a broken arrow as shown above. *The broken arrow justifies all dominant resolutions down a half step*.

The expected resolution for all configurations of Mixolydian chord scales (including altered and whole-tone) is down a perfect 5th; the chord scale for a substitute dominant can not be Mixolydian. The other dominant chord scale shown in the beginning section of this book is *Lydian ♭7*. It is the appropriate chord scale for substitute dominants and by comparing the notes of the Lydian ♭7 scale with the dominant chord for which it substitutes, their common chord scale relationship is revealed:

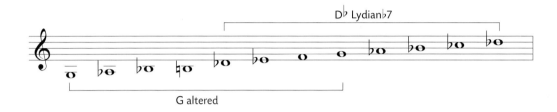

The chord scale for the substitute dominant contains the same notes as the altered scale for the dominant. Although these chords share the same function, they can not freely be exchanged in melodic situations where the melody represents *unaltered* pitches from the dominant's Mixolydian scale. Chords using Mixolydian or any form of altered Mixolydian are expected to resolve down a perfect 5th; chords using Lydian ♭7 are expected to resolve with root motion *not* down a perfect 5th.

Of the twelve possible dominant chords, six pairs substitute for one other. Included are the primary dominant V7 and its subV7 as well as subV7/II, subV7/IV, subV7/V as substitutes for the respective secondary dominants:

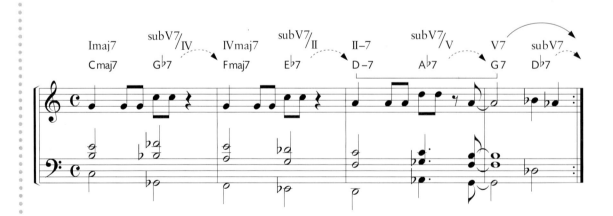

There are two important things to recognize in the last two measures of the above example. The subV7/V is *interpolated* between the II–7 and its related V7. The subV7 is interpolated between the V7 and delays its resolution to tonic. Both interpolations are typical of jazz influenced progressions.

There are many alternatives for a Mixolydian scale without alterations. However, there are no alternative possibilities for a Lydian♭7 scale excepting the use of Lydian♭7(♯9), if the expected resolution is to a diatonic chord which contains a major 3rd. (The ♯9 represents the resolution chord's major 3rd.) This is an instance where ♭9 and ♯9 *can not coexist* because ♭9 has no relationship to the chord of resolution. Lydian♭7(♯9) *can be an alternative chord scale for* subV7 of Imaj7, IVmaj7 or V7. (The symmetric dominant chord scale is also an alternative for the Mixolydian and the Lydian♭7 scales. It will be discussed at length later.)

Omitted from the substitute secondary dominant list is subV7/VII (again), subV7/III and subV7/VI. By observing the characteristics of substitute dominants, explanation for some of these omissions can be seen:

- They are nondiatonic structures.
- They function diatonically.
- The roots are nondiatonic.
- The expected resolution target chord is diatonic, down a half step.
- The chord scales are nondiatonic.
- They appear on weak stress points.

SubV7/III has a diatonic root. It is most often heard as a IV7. This subdominant functioning chord will be seen later in blues. A substitute dominant of the VII–7(♭5) would be rooted on V7/IV in the key. That leaves subV7/VI. Usually the ♭VII7 chord is expected to resolve up a whole step to the tonic Imaj7. The function here is not dominant and will be discussed at length in the minor key chapter. In rare situations involving harmonic rhythm, it is possible to find subV7/III or subV7/VI on extremely weak stress locations or following the secondary dominant for which they substitute:

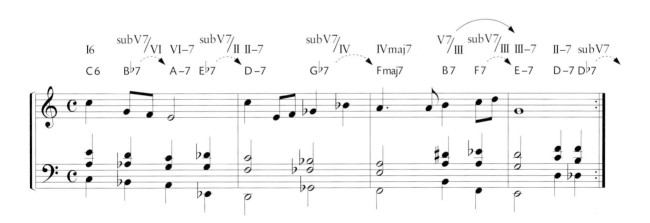

This example also contains a delayed resolution. Both the V7/III and its substitute have a common resolution to the III–7 chord. The V7/III forces the F7 to function as subV7/III.

Just as the chord scale for IVmaj7 is effected when V7/IV precedes it, if subV7/IV resolves to IVmaj7 the chord scale for the IV chord is Ionian.

Another possibility of deriving substitute dominants is based on V7 with a lowered 5th. In general the real 7(♭5) is rare but it was featured a lot by Thelonious Monk. His compositions and improvisations often contain 7(♭5) as well as +7 chords. Those chords are closely related to each other; both are based on a symmetrical chord scale – whole-tone. In lead sheets the 7(♭5) is often an incorrectly spelled 7(♯11) chord (with the appropriate Lydian♭7 chord scale).

SubV7(♭5) represents the second inversion of V7(♭5). Because of this relationship they also use the same chord scale:

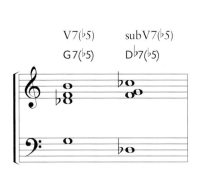

Monk's original changes of his classic composition "'Round Midnight" contain some subV7(♭5) chords:

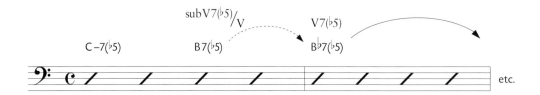

Although there is no such term as substitute dominants known in traditional harmony, composers of the 18th century utilized the effect of approaching the dominant or tonic chromatically. Classified as Augmented Sixth Chords, they accomplish the function of substitute dominants. The characteristic interval between bass and top note gives an augmented sixth, hence the name, but it is indistinguishable from a minor seventh in sound. So why augmented sixth chord?

Augmented sixth chords are the result of inverted dominant functioning chords with a lowered 5th producing an additional leading tone to a diatonic chord. In the case of an augmented sixth chord leading to V7, the lowered 5th of V7/V gives the new root (which is very familiar to the diatonic, because it represents the ♭6 scale degree = subdominant minor) producing an augmented sixth with the 3rd of V7/V. This chord is also known as French augmented sixth chord (Fr+6).

It may be found in the music of Mozart, Chopin, Verdi, Schubert and other composers (especially of the 19th century). The following example also contains a related II–7 chord which will be discussed at the end of this chapter:

SCHUBERT, OP. 90, IMPROMPTUS NO. 1

In traditional music augmented sixth chords occur mostly as dominant functioning chords leading to the primary dominant, respectively tonic. They may appear in different inversions, but they always contain the 3rd and 7th of the corresponding dominant chord.

The most prominent augmented sixth chord is the German augmented sixth chord (Ger+6). It is derived from V7(♭9), with VII°7 representing the upper structure of V7(♭9) (refer to *Diminished Seventh Chords*). Again the 5th is lowered and serves as the root:

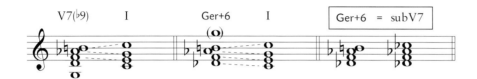

Spelled enharmonically this chord represents a dominant seventh chord structure. In jazz context this type of chord is not considered an augmented 6th chord anymore but a substitute dominant chord, which serves a more independent function and may substitute not only for V7 and V7/V, but also for V7/II, V7/IV, in rare cases also for V7/III and V7/VI. (Refer to the beginning of this chapter.)

The following example by W. A. Mozart shows a deceptive resolution of the Ger+6 chord (=subV7) which was expected to resolve to II–:

W. A. MOZART,
KV 332

Sequential Substitute Dominants

Sequential substitute dominant motion is not as common as sequential dominant motion. The chord movement during sequential dominant activity follows the cycle of 5ths and is shown with solid arrows:

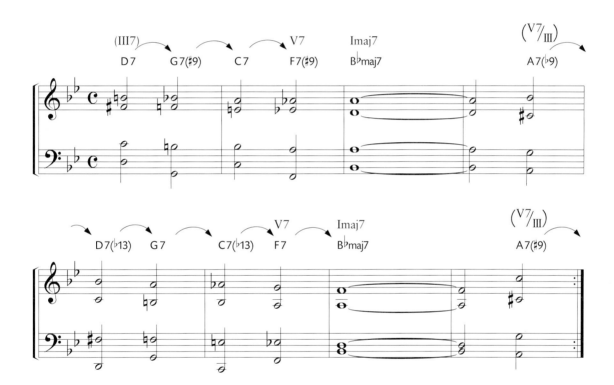

The chord movement during sequential substitute dominant activity has more a chromatic sound as opposed to a dominant sound but the analysis using broken arrows will justify the motions:

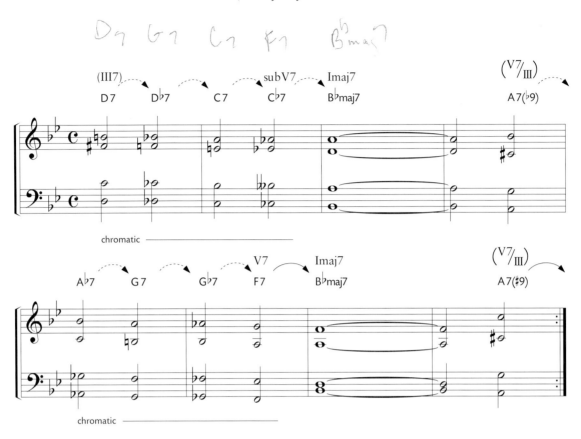

Compare both examples visually then compare the sounds. The chord scale for each chord is determined by either chromatic sound or dominant function. A choice must be made based on the chords which surround each dominant chord. The chord scale choice may be based on the first or last chord of the series.

In the first 4 measures, the C♭7 is functioning as subV7 with a Lydian♭7 scale; the chromatic sounds leading to it will sound chromatic if they are also Lydian♭7. Conversely, the first chord of the series sounds like a sequential dominant using a Mixolydian scale; the dominants which follow could be chromatic Mixolydian scales.

In the second line of the example, the F7 functions as Mixolydian V7 and therefore a correct choice for the preceding chromatic dominants is also Mixolydian. But, the first chord of the series has a nondiatonic root and uses a Lydian♭7 chord scale; all the chromatic chords which follow could be chromatic Lydian♭7.

This liberal choice of chord scales falls under the heading of "artistic judgement" again. Where so many choices exist, you will usually be in the area of non-functional harmonies. More about this later, but, if one perceives the progression as dominant motion, then use dominant functioning chord scales; if one perceives chromatic (non-functional) motion, use chromatic chord scales.

A more common setting for functional sequential substitute dominant motion is found where they appear interpolated prior to the resolution of their tritone substitute chord:

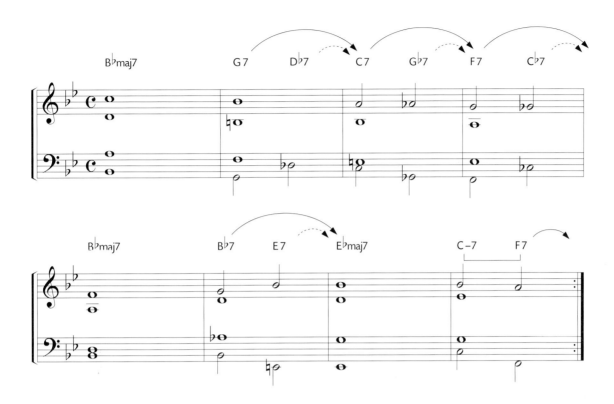

The analysis is incomplete above in order to better see the dominant chords resolutions. It is more common to hear the substitute dominant following the sequential dominant. This type chord progression is often heard during the turnxaround prior to the repeating of a phrase (listen to your favorite bass player):

The following excerpt shows the application of sequential substitute dominants in traditional music. The subV7 chords were traditionally written as German augmented sixth chords. Note that the melody implies Lydian♭7 as the appropriate chord scale:

F. Schubert,
op. 83, 2

Woe's me! Where am I?

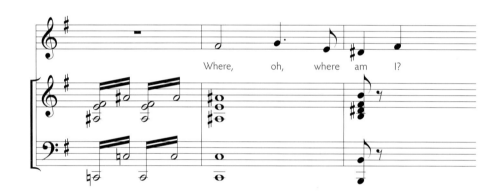

Where, oh, where am I?

TUNES TO ANALYZE FOR SUBSTITUTE DOMINANTS

"One Note Samba"

"The Girl From Ipanema" (A section)

"Peace" (It's difficult!)

"Turn Out the Stars" (Bill Evans – the last 3rd)

"Sophisticated Lady"

Any dominant chord *may be preceded by its related* II–7 except I7 and IV7 in the blues. This use of II–7 V7 is ultra-typical of jazz and styles influenced by jazz:

A –7	D 7	D –7	G 7	G –7	C 7	C –7	F 7

F –7	B♭7	B♭–7	E♭7	E♭–7	A♭7	A♭–7	D♭7

D♭–7	G♭7	F♯–7	B 7	B –7	E 7	E –7	A 7

The bracket is always used to show the II–7 V7 relationship. The addition of the II–7 will complicate the harmonic rhythm as well as the analysis of the progression. With the inclusion of the II–7 the direction the chords may take is expanded immensely. The related II–7 chord may also be diatonic and represent *a dual function chord*:

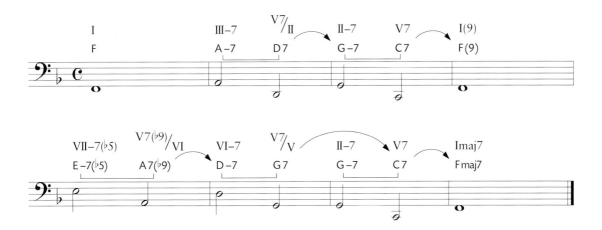

The dual function –7 chord may use the appropriate diatonic scale or a Dorian scale to reflect the relationship to the dominant chord. The use of a Dorian scale has potential for destroying any deceptive sound for the dominant. This must be considered prior to the chord scale choice for the –7 chord.

The [___] may appear with alterations to both chords or to either chord. All the following combinations represent the sound of [___] :

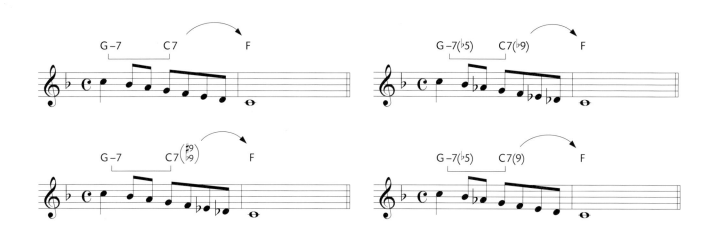

In order for the relationship to sound as a [___], the harmonic rhythm must be II–7 — *strong stress*, V7 — *weak stress*. This is an absolute must for the listener. A prime example are the changes in the beginning of the tune "I Got It Bad and That Ain't Good" by Duke Ellington.

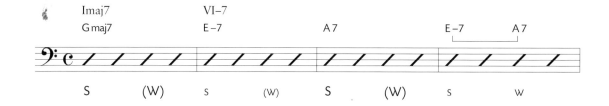

The chord in the second measure is VI–7; in the 4th measure it is a related II–7 although the E–7 A7 appears in both locations. The harmonic rhythm is what forces the issue.

The [___] may repeat itself and not effect the function of either chord. The chords from the beginning of another Duke tune "Satin Doll" can demonstrate this (as does "Speak Low):

Sequential dominant progressions that include the related II–7 chords may become very complicated for the listener. In most situations where the related II–7 chords appear before the sequential dominant chord, it is difficult, but possible, to hear diatonic functions for the –7 chord. This is how Dave Brubeck's song "In Your Own Sweet Way" starts:

It could be heard and analyzed as a sequential dominant progression:

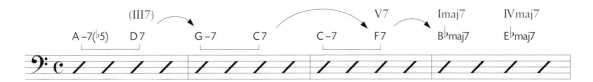

or as secondary dominants and dual function –7 chords:

or beginning in the relative G minor:

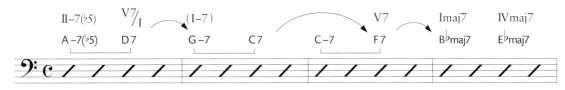

(Change of function from tonic minor to related II–7.)

The choice of analysis is yours and will be dictated to the listener. With the availability of the related II–7 chord, *any sequential dominant may resolve to another sequential dominant's related II–7.*

Another very common occurrence is for the II–7 chord to be heard interpolated prior to a resolution to its dominant. The continuation of Duke's tune "I Got It Bad and That Ain't Good" can illustrate this:

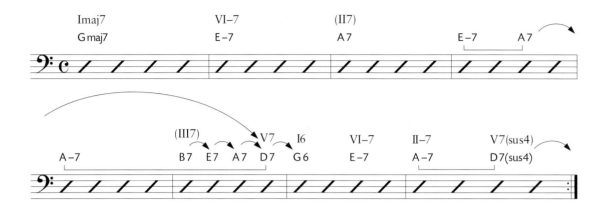

The II–7 (A–7) is interpolated prior to the resolution of A7 to D7 and, there is a sequential dominant progression interpolated between the └────┘ .

The related II–7 chords of the secondary dominants have dual functions except the –7 built on V which is most often the related II–7 of V7/IV. (V–7 will later be shown as a special cadential chord.) The –7 chord built on ♯IV is usually ♯IV–7(♭5) (the ♭5 is tonic of the key) and will receive a full treatment later.

The related II–7 chords of the substitute dominants are nondiatonically rooted. With the related II–7 chords of the dominant and its substitute, a four-way relationship can exist:

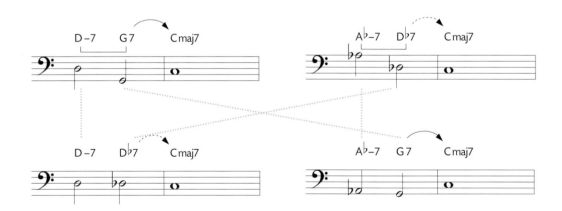

All four of these chords have an interrelationship. *Either of the dominants may be preceded with the other dominant's related II–7 chord.*

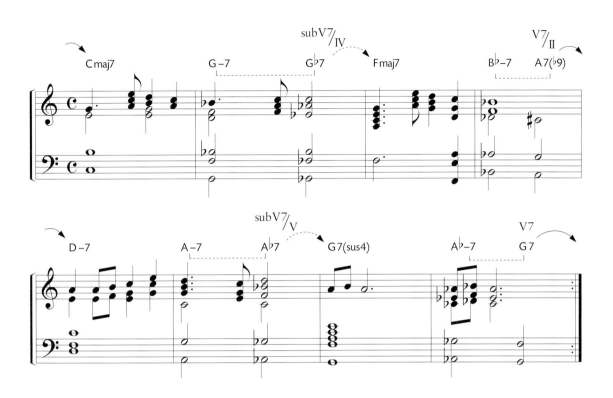

The ⌐------⌐ is used to show the half step relationship between the –7 and the dominant. A *solid* arrow or bracket indicates root motion down a perfect 5th:

A *broken* arrow or bracket indicates root motion down a half step:

Both –7 chords exist because of their relationship to their related dominant chord. Although the dominant chords are substitutes for each other, these –7 chords are not. Examine the Dorian chord scales for the related II–7 chords:

D Dorian:

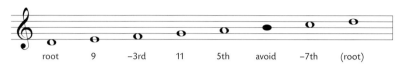

| root | 9 | –3rd | 11 | 5th | avoid | –7th | (root) |

Ab Dorian:

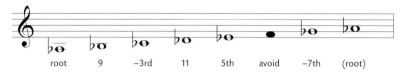

| root | 9 | –3rd | 11 | 5th | avoid | –7th | (root) |

If both scales are combined, the result will be a chromatic scale with 6 pitches available for one of the Dorian chord's scales and the other 6 for the other Dorian chord. Where one works, the other does not. Therefore, the related II–7 chords for substitute dominants *cannot* substitute for each other. However, where a melodic situation occurs where one chord will not work, the other chord must work:

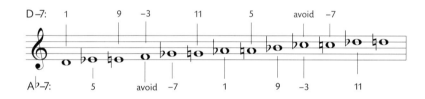

Before leaving the subject of II–7 V7s, it is very common to use Dorian-Mixolydian when a ⌐___⌐ occurs, even in a sequential substitute dominant situation (as opposed to the use of Lydian♭7 for the dominant). The Dorian-Mixolydian scales represent a unified element because both scales contain the same pitches. Here again an artistic judgement is forced upon the player/writer.

TUNES TO ANALYZE FOR RELATED II–7 CHORDS

"Dreamsville"

"I'm All Smiles"

"Satin Doll"

"I Got It Bad and That Ain't Good"

"One Note Samba"

"My Little Boat"

"In Your Own Sweet Way"

4
Minor Key Harmony

MODAL INTERCHANGE AND SUBDOMINANT MINOR

The most common *modal interchange* occurs by borrowing natural minor chords for major key progressions:

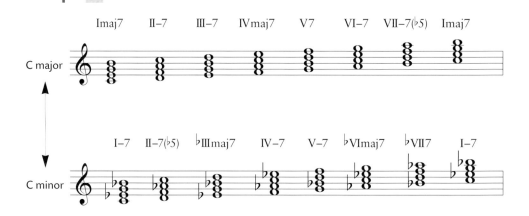

The chords that are transplanted from the parallel natural minor key can be categorized in their major key setting as tonic minor or nontonic.

The character note of natural minor is scale degree ♭6. The tonic minor chords do not contain this pitch as a chord tone; the nontonic sounds contain ♭6 as a chord tone. In the primary key of I major, the natural minor character note ♭6 is the −3rd of the subdominant IV− chord. The nontonic natural minor chords can be heard as functionally sounding like *subdominant minor* chords in the primary major key. The remaining three chords are functionally tonic minor sounds in the major key:

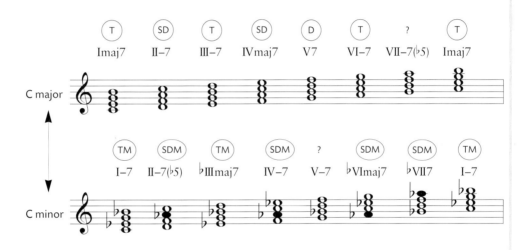

The I−7 is the strongest tonic minor. ♭IIImaj7 is also a strong tonic minor sound. Both are common in major key progressions. V−7 is very weak because the −3rd scale degree of natural minor is an avoided ♭13:

The chord scales for the modal interchange chords from natural minor will reflect their use in a major key or their origin in a minor key or a combination of both considerations.

The tonic minor chord scales usually contain the natural 6 scale degree since ♭6 represents the functional sound of the subdominant minor chords. The **I–7** chord is most often a *Dorian* chord scale with 13 as an available tension. The natural 13 reinforces the major key while the minor scale implies the minor key:

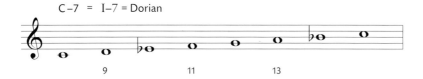

The ♭IIImaj7 chord is usually a Lydian scale. The ♯11 holds the progression to the key of I major – not implying movement into the natural minor key's related major (key of ♭III):

If the **V–7** is functioning as a tonic minor chord from natural minor, its chord scale is *Aeolian*. However, it most often occurs as a chord borrowed from the key of *Mixolydian* because of its close relationship to the tonic chord in that key. A chord closely related to V–7 is ♭VIImaj7 that can also be seen as a Mixolydian modal interchange chord. The chord scale for ♭VIImaj7 is *Lydian* to reflect its nontonic function:

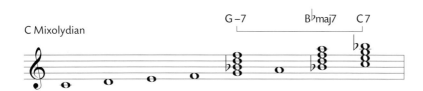

In normal circumstances the V–7 chord would be analyzed as the related II–7 of V7/IV, not as V–7, and therefore use a *Dorian* scale (avoid 13). If the function is truly V–7, the chord will be cadencing to tonic major or minor and also use a *Dorian* scale as a modal interchange chord from Mixolydian ("Dreamsville). The 13 is available in this context:

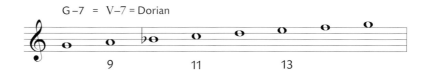

It is not unusual to find the V–7 as a hybrid structure or the upper structure in a I7(sus4) chord ("Dolphin Dance" by Herbie Hancock or "Never Can Say Goodbye" as done by the Jackson 5):

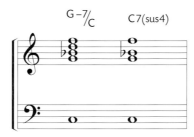

The primary subdominant minor chord is the IV–7 chord. Its subdominant minor color is dependent upon the character note ♭6 of the key. It can also appear as a IV–6 or IV–(maj7) even though the major 7th represents the major 3rd scale degree of the major key. All forms of the IV– chord function as subdominant minor:

| IV–7 | Imaj7 | IV–6 | Imaj7 | IV–(maj7) | Imaj7 |
| F–7 | Cmaj7 | F–6 | Cmaj7 | F–(maj7) | Cmaj7 |

The subdominant minor chords are unstable and have the potential for movement to either tonic minor or tonic major. Therefore, cadential motion in major key may be *subdominant minor,* along with *subdominant* or *dominant,* with resolution to either tonic major or tonic minor.

Classical music also used different types of subdominant chords. The IV major chord with an added 6th (sixte ajoutée) as harmonic dissonance was employed around 1600. Like the minor 7th of the dominant seventh chord, which developed around 1700, harmonic dissonances originated as neighbor notes or passing tones. The subdominant minor chord with an added maj 6th (IV−6) or maj 7th (IV−(maj7)) was hardly ever used in traditional tonal music. While the IV−6, which was avoided for its tritone between 3rd and 6th, can be found in Bach's music, the IV−(maj7) occurs only in the music of the 19th century.

J. Brahms, In stiller Nacht

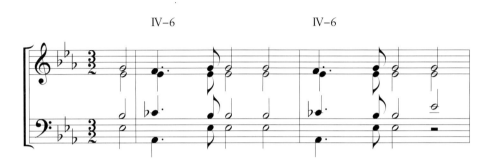

F. Schubert, Moments musicaux, op. 94, No. 6

The following example shows the different types of the IV chord used in traditional music between 1650 and 1900:

* Until circa 1700 those chords were understood as subdominant chords with the 6th substituting for the 5th and not as an inversion of a II chord (refer to *A Brief History of Harmony*). The chord marked N6, containing a minor 6th, was a special alternative for the IV− chord with major 6th. It will be discussed in detail.

Composers of the 19th century favored the use of different diatonic nondominant seventh chords including IVmaj7 and IV–7.

The different forms of the IV– chord have differing options for their chord scales. The IV–7 chord is a Dorian chord scale. Natural 13 is available with care because it will tend to make the chord sound like the IV–6 chord which follows:

IV–6 may be either a *Dorian (avoid ♭7* – usually due to melodic content) or *melodic minor* with scale degree 3 of the major key available as maj7. This helps define the major key. The same chord scale is used for the IV–(maj7) chord:

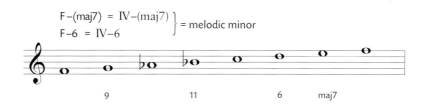

The basic chord structure of subdominant minor chords contains the characteristic ♭6 of the key. But some of these chords may also function differently and therefore require closer examination.

The II–7(♭5) chord is most often heard preceding the V7(♭9) as a two chord (⎣___⎤) element. Both chords are borrowed from harmonic minor, not from natural minor:

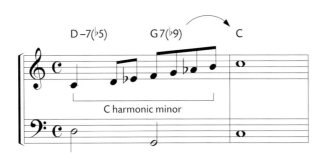

It is uncommon to find the II–7(♭5) standing alone as a cadential chord from natural minor. Because it appears prior to the V7, the expectation is for the II–7(♭5) to progress to V7(♭9) prior to a cadence to tonic major or tonic minor. Examples can be found with II–7(♭5) functioning as a subdominant minor chord, but they are unusual. It is most often the related II–7(♭5) of V7(♭9). The Locrian – Mixolydian (♭9, ♭13) chord scales will reflect their harmonic minor origin.

♭VII7 uses a *Lydian♭7* scale most of the time, reflecting the implication of minor but its use in major, and its expected root motion to tonic major that is not down a perfect 5th. (Both ♭VI7 and ♭VII7 are typical examples of *dominant chords without dominant function*.):

However, ♭VII7 has a ⎣___⎤ relationship with the primary subdominant minor chord, IV–7. As an element, the IV–7 ♭VII7, when heard or analyzed with a ⎣___⎤ may use *Dorian – Mixolydian* to suggest the sound of ⎣___⎤ and, the resolution may be down a perfect 5th to ♭IIImaj7:

The chord scale for ♭VImaj7 is *Lydian* reflecting its nontonic function:

The voice leading of the ♭VI chord as a subdominant minor modal interchange chord has resulted in another altered subdominant chord. The ♭VI7 chord can be heard as a cadential chord moving to tonic major or tonic minor:

Like subV7/V the nondominant ♭VI7 chord is also related to the traditional German augmented sixth chord (refer to the previous chapter). While the dominant functioning Ger+6 (subV7/V) is derived from a diminished chord with secondary dominant function (upper structure of V7(♭9)/V), the nondominant Ger+6 (♭VI7) is derived from the same diminished chord with chromatic function (enharmonically spelled). Although the Ger+6 chord most often has dominant function, it may be found as a nondominant cadential chord as in the following example:

F. Schubert, op. 83, 3

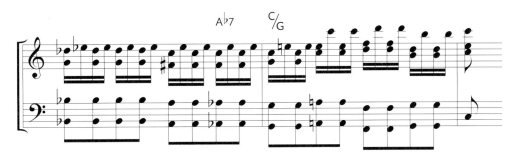

The 7th of A♭7
is spelled as an
augmented 6th.

Sometimes the nondominant Ger+6 chord was spelled incorrectly (on purpose or by mistake like in the previous example). Since it does not appear very often, the spelling of the common dominant Ger+6 was applied. (Note that the Ger+6 chord also has dominant function if the second inversion of the tonic is a suspension of the primary dominant chord to which it progresses; this is typical for a classical cadence.) If the nondominant Ger+6 moves to I major the correct spelling includes, besides an augmented 6th, an ascending chromatic approach to the 3rd of the tonic chord (doubly augmented fourth). This chord is sometimes called Swiss augmented sixth chord to distinguish it from the dominant functioning Ger+6 chord:

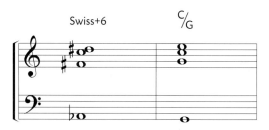

In contemporary usage both the subV7/V and ♭VI7 chord are spelled the same as a dominant seventh chord structure built on the ♭VI scale degree. Notation based on voice leading, as in the case of the traditional Ger+6 and Swiss+6 chord, is not applicable for chord symbols and generally avoided for easy reading purpose.

In jazz the ♭VI7 is treated as an altered subdominant minor chord or Blues chord (refer to *Dominant Chords with Special Functions*) if it progresses cadentially (as in "Bye Bye Blues" or "Out of Nowhere"). If the chord is progressing as a secondary substitute dominant, it will be subV7/V. Usually the distinction is based on context. Analysis symbols show the appropriate function:

If the ♭VI7 is a cadence chord without dominant function, (its expectation is for root motion other than down a perfect 5th) it uses a *Lydian ♭7* chord scale. If it has substitute dominant function as subV7/V it also uses *Lydian ♭7*:

If the II–7(♭5) appears as a subdominant minor chord, often ♭IImaj7 follows. ♭IImaj7 also can be categorized as a *subdominant minor chord* progressing cadentially to tonic major or minor. It will later be shown as a modal interchange chord from parallel Phrygian.

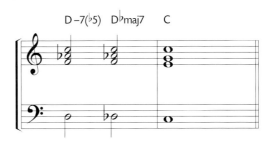

The ♭IImaj7 is not considered a II–7(♭5) with a chromatically lowered root. In functional harmony all chord tones may be altered except the root which is the chord's basis.

The origin of the ♭IImaj7 chord traces back to the 17th century. It developed from IV– with the minor 6th substituting for the 5th. Primarily used in minor tunes, this chord was an alternative for IV–6 (which would produce a tritone between 3rd and 6th and was therefore avoided). It can be found in the works of Neapolitan composers, especially in the Neapolitan Opera, hence the name Neapolitan (Sixth) chord (N6). Many of these composers were active throughout Europe, and by the middle of the 17th century this chord was an established harmonic idiom. Contrary to today's analysis the N6 was considered a IV– chord and not a form of a II chord. In the later 18th and in the 19th century the Neapolitan chord was employed also in major context and with increasing frequency in root position (N) producing more stability and independence. The N6 like the ♭IImaj7 chord have strong subdominant character progressing to tonic major/minor or to the primary dominant chord (traditional music).

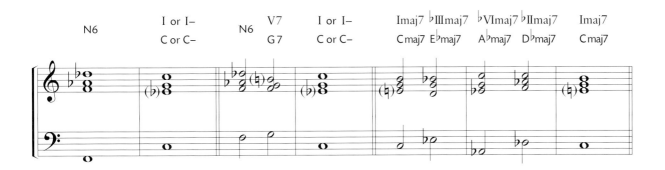

The last three measures show a turnaround as in "Lady Bird" including modal interchange chords, especially subdominant minor chords. (Subdominant minor cadences produce a guide tone line which includes scale degree ♭6 resolving to the *5th* of the tonic chord.)

Due to the close relationship between the keys of I major and ♭III major, it is very common to find tunes moving freely between them ("Softly" or "On Green Dolphin Street"). The composer's/arranger's/player's choice of chord scales is what makes this movement to the new key possible. When subdominant minor function is involved, there is only an implication of a modulation to the related key (as in "Night and Day" or "You Go To My Head").

SUMMARY OF SUBDOMINANT MINOR CHORDS

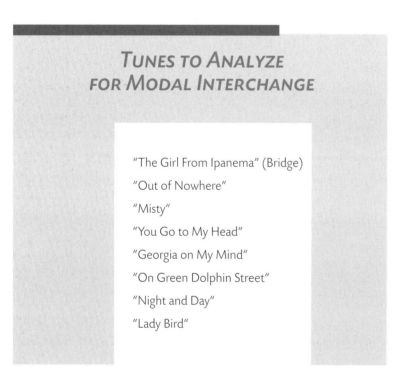

TUNES TO ANALYZE
FOR MODAL INTERCHANGE

"The Girl From Ipanema" (Bridge)

"Out of Nowhere"

"Misty"

"You Go to My Head"

"Georgia on My Mind"

"On Green Dolphin Street"

"Night and Day"

"Lady Bird"

Minor key harmony is as complex as major key harmony. Chord progressions in minor are more diatonic oriented though. While the major scale never changes, the minor scale is variable, which gives more possibilities to create diatonic chords. The difference lies in the second tetrachord (second half of the scale). Scale degrees 1 through 5 are unchangeable, but the 6th and 7th degrees are either major or minor. (Scale degree ♭5 is often found as a melody pitch in minor key – see measure 6 of "Yesterdays.") The tonal material of nine tones gives the possibility of four different scale configurations:

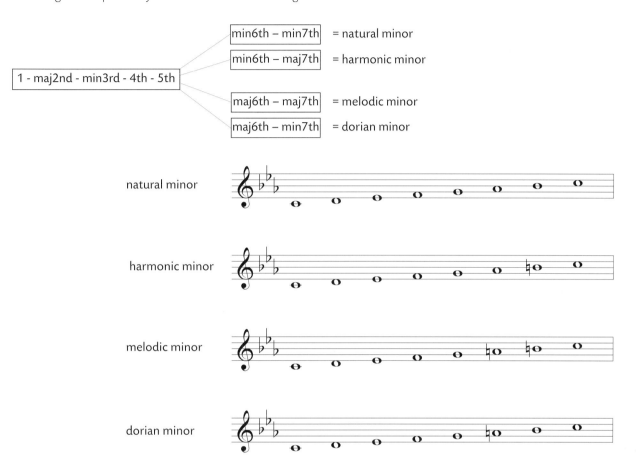

- Natural minor is *natural* to the key signature.
- Natural minor is *not* identified as Aeolian in order to distinguish it from Aeolian as a mode.
- Harmonic and melodic minors are not diatonic to a key signature.
- Harmonic minor has the 7th scale degree raised from natural minor for *harmonic* purposes. It contains a leading tone which produces a dominant V (or V7) chord. Hence the name:

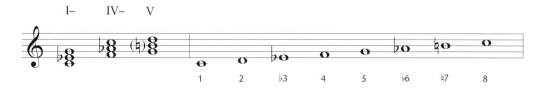

- Melodic minor has the 6th degree raised from harmonic minor for melodic *purposes.*
- Dorian minor has the 6th degree raised from natural minor making it diatonic to a different key signature (two flats in the above circumstance).
- Of all the minor tonalities, only dorian minor uses a modal adjective.

Traditional harmony mostly deals with three different minor scales: Natural, harmonic, and melodic minor, although dorian minor is an important tonal source for transitions and modulations.

Concerning the traditional interpretation of the melodic minor scale: It is just a guide line and *not* a rule that maj6th and maj7th appear in succession only in ascending and min6th and min7th only in descending lines (natural minor). The contemporary use of the melodic minor scale contains the maj6th and the maj7th ascending *and* descending. But this appearance can be found in several examples of traditional music too:

J. S. Bach, Well-Tempered Clavier, Book I:

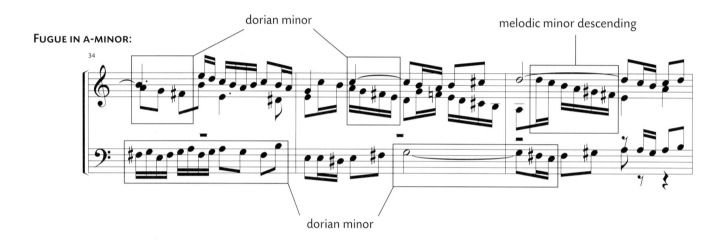

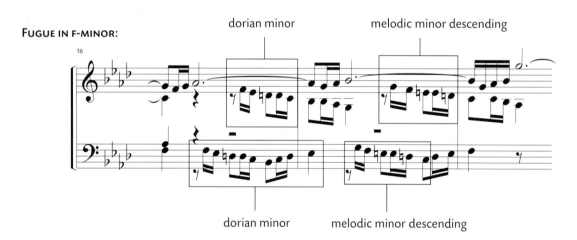

MINOR CHORDS AND MODAL INTERCHANGE

It is possible to find contemporary songs which are exclusively in one minor tonality but they are exceeded in number by tunes using chords from any or all of the minor key sources. Because of the variable 6th and 7th scale degree, every minor scale contributes another set of chords. About three times more chords are available in minor key than in major. Some of them occur more frequently than others. They are available through *modal interchange* (borrowing chords from parallel tonalities; *mode* here refers to a functional context). *Modal interchange is very common to minor key progressions.*

Note: Some of the Roman numerals in the following list contain a flat. This is necessary in minor key to show the root position for the 6th and 7th scale degrees. The ♭ indicates "lowered" and will be used for the diatonic ♭III, ♭VI and ♭VII chords.

The diatonic chords in natural minor are:

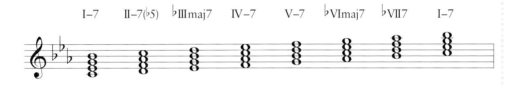

The harmonic minor diatonic chords are:

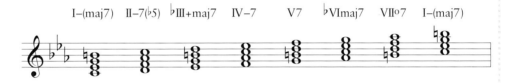

The melodic minor chords are:

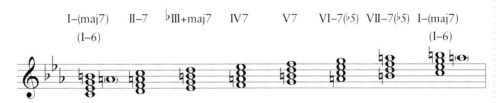

The dorian minor diatonic chords are:

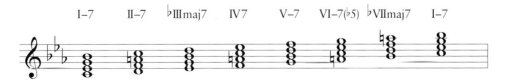

- The I– chord in melodic minor is usually a I–6 to distinguish it from the I–(maj7) of harmonic minor.

- In most cases the V7 is used (instead of V–7), because of its primary dominant function.

- The dorian minor tonality is most significant for its melodic importance. The ♭VIImaj7 is the only chord it contributes for modal interchange. However, the I–7 chord scale is very important as will be seen when viewing all the chord scales.

- Sometimes only triads are used (tonic) to get more functional stability or to initiate a line cliché (refer to the end of this chapter).

Here are the minor key diatonic chords available through modal interchange:

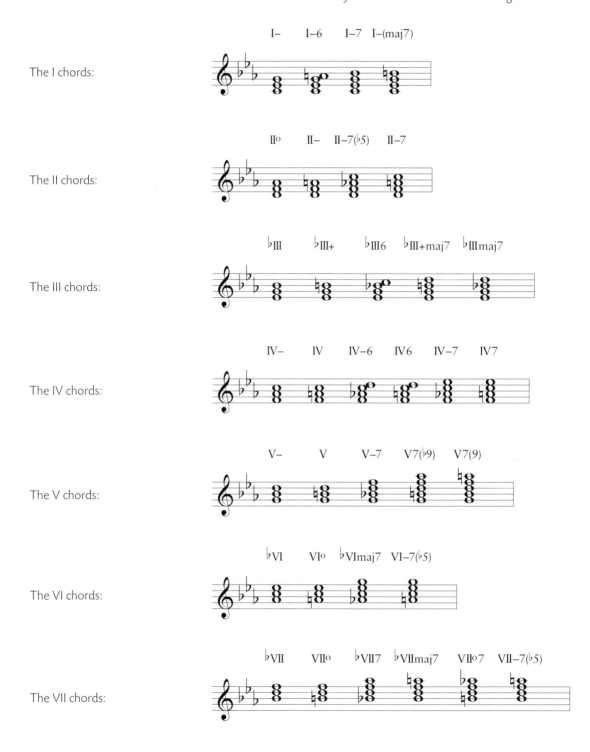

In the above listing:

- the –6 and 6 chords are alternatives for their maj7 and –(maj7) counter-parts;

- the –6, –(maj7), +maj7 and °7 chords are not found diatonic to major key;

- there are dominant chord structures built on IV, V and ♭VII but only the V7 chord has primary dominant function as V7/I;

- V–7 is *not* a dominant functioning chord, but may cadence to tonic;

- the VII°7 chord may have dominant function in minor. (It is the upper extension of the V7(♭9));

- although not diatonic to any minor key, the chords ♭IImaj7, IV–(maj7) and ♭VI7 (refer to *Modal Interchange and Subdominant Minor*) will be found in minor key situations as cadential chords:

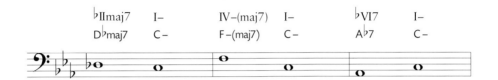

In addition to the use of modal interchange between minor key sources, in minor keys it is common to find:

- secondary dominant motion,

- substitute dominants,

- sequential dominants, sequential substitute dominants, and

- related II–7 and II–7(♭5) chords.

KEY RELATIONSHIPS

The traditional definitions are still applicable for *relative* and *parallel* key relationships. Relative keys share the *same diatonic*; parallel keys share the *same tonal center*. Since natural minor and its relative major key share the same diatonic, the stress placement of chords and melodic cadences determines which is in effect at any given moment.

There are also examples of minor key tunes which move from the minor key into the parallel major key. (Just as the traditional use of "tierce de Picardie". An example is "Alone Together" which has a cadence to Imaj7 at the end of the first two A sections but stays in minor at the end.)

Less common are minor key tunes utilizing relative and parallel key relationships. "Lament" can be heard as moving from tonic minor into the parallel major then to the parallel major's relative minor. It ends in the parallel major key. Within minor tunes, the common key relationships are:

- in the key of I minor only (C minor),
- in the key of I minor and its relative major (C minor – E♭ major),
- in the key of I minor and its parallel major (C minor – C major),
- in the key of I minor, and its parallel major, and the parallel major's relative minor (C minor – C major – A minor),
- in the key of I minor, and its relative major, and the relative major's parallel minor (C minor – E♭ major – E♭ minor).

The last relationship is not as common as those above.

The basic considerations used in determining the chord scales for major key related chords apply to chords found in minor keys. The diatonic chords use diatonic chord scales. However, there is much more freedom of choice because the 6th and 7th scale degrees may be either natural or raised. Avoid note criteria remains the same as major key except for the Dorian scale, allowing the use of tension 13, especially on the I–7 chord. This important tension inclusion is indicative of the sound of dorian minor.

The potential diatonic I– chord scales are:

- I–7 .... Dorian or Aeolian.

- I–6 .... Dorian (avoid ♭7) or melodic minor.

- I–(maj7) .... melodic minor or harmonic minor.

- I– (triad) .... either a scale using degrees 1 through 5 (all the common pitches from the above scales) or any of the above scales assuming the melody conforms to the choice.

- I–7 .... Phrygian is a potential scale, especially if the melody is phrygian minor (unusual).

In the tonic minor scale choices, the 11th degree stands out as a sound associated with non-tonic and as such, its use requires care. (On the I–(maj7), 11 creates a tritone with the major 7th. This tritone relationship with the 3rd or 7th of the chord is reserved for dominant function.)

The remaining diatonic chord scales use the same pattern of choice. The commonly used chord scales follow with other options available based on the minor key criteria:

II–7 · · · · · · · · · · · Phrygian or Dorian (♭2)

II–7(♭5) · · · · · · · · · Locrian

♭IIImaj7 · · · · · · · · · Lydian or Ionian

IV–7 · · · · · · · · · · · Dorian

IV7 (V7/♭VII) · · · · · Lydian ♭7 or Mixolydian

V7(♭9) · · · · · · · · · · Mixolydian (♭9, ♯9, ♭13)
                            (This is a composite of most minor key pitches.)

V7 · · · · · · · · · · · · Mixolydian (♭13)

V–7 · · · · · · · · · · · Aeolian

♭VImaj7 · · · · · · · · · Lydian

VI–7(♭5) · · · · · · · · · Locrian or Locrian (♮9)

♭VII7 (V7/♭III) · · · · · Lydian (♭7) or Mixolydian

♭VIImaj7 · · · · · · · · · Ionian

VII°7 · · · · · · · · · · · (rarely used) The chord scale is a displacement of the harmonic minor scale.

Most of the non-tonic chord scales, and therefore the resulting available tensions, are drawn from either natural minor or dorian minor. As a minor tonality, dorian minor is not important as a source for diatonic chords but, along with natural minor, is important as a basis for the pitches associated with most minor key melodies. The chord scales used for the tonic I– chord may represent *any form of minor scale*.

Dominant chords similar in function to those found in major key harmony (secondary dominants, substitute dominants, sequential dominants, sequential substitute dominants, related II–7 chords) have chord scales which meet necessary criteria for their construction:

- Chords with diatonic orientation use diatonic non-chord tones.

- Dominant chords which have expected resolutions down a perfect fifth use some form of Mixolydian chord scale.

- Dominant chords which have expected resolutions other then down a perfect fifth use a Lydian♭7 chord scale.

- Basically, if the root of a chord is diatonic, think diatonic for the chord scale construction; if the root of a chord is nondiatonic, the construction of the chord scale needs a logical justification.

- The diatonic pitches associated with minor tonalities include the natural and raised 6th and 7th scale degrees of the key.

Because the 6th and 7th scale degrees in minor are natural or raised, the root of many of the dominant chords functioning in the key may be both a perfect fifth and a half step above a diatonic pitch; at the same time an expectation for resolution *down a perfect 5th* (Mixolydian with or without alterations), or resolution *not down a perfect 5th* (Lydian♭7).

Some interesting scale choices are created by using the composite minor scale:

C– composite scale:

E7 (V7/VI) in C– could be any of the following scales using non-chord tones from the composite minor scale:

E7 = Mixolydian (♭9, ♯9, ♭13)

E7 = Mixolydian (♭9, ♯9, ♯11, ♭13)

or:

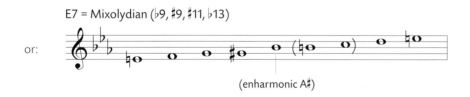

(enharmonic A♯)

E7 = altered

or:

E7 (SubV7/♭III) in C– could be either:

E7 = Lydian♭7

or:

E7 = Lydian♭7(♯9)

OR: the scale for E7 (with a questionable function in C–) might combine all the virtues above and use a chord scale form of:

E7 = symmetric dominant

This scale can been seen as symmetric half step, whole step. There are no avoid notes because all the pitches meet the available pitch criteria for a dominant function. This scale is often referred to as one of the two *symmetric diminished* chord scales. (Refer to the listing of scales in the first chapter.) However, more correctly, this particular form of symmetric scale relates to dominant function and should be considered a *symmetric dominant* chord scale or it can be called a *combination dominant*. (The lower half is altered (♭9, ♯9); the top half is Lydian♭7 (♯11, 13).)

The many choices of scales available in minor key may appear almost endless, however, the truth is there are many more scales that are appropriate for use in minor keys than for major key.

The following tune has been forced to contain typical minor key chord progressions:

Common minor key traits:

Typically, the minor tonality is established immediately with the tonic chord stressed.

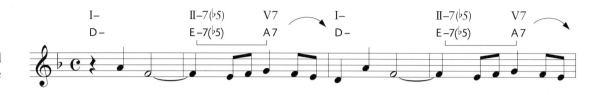

Secondary dominants of II, IV, and V predominate.

Sequential dominants (all diatonically rooted) often occur and, as in major key, ultimately resolve to a diatonic chord.

Unlike major key, the secondary dominant of V may appear on a strong stress where the II−7 would normally be (as in the first A section).

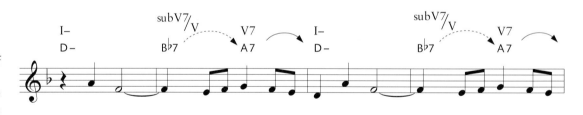

Nondominant cadences from the diatonic ♭VII7 are common.

Line cliches are frequently found in minor key chord progressions. The single line's movement creates the impression of harmonic activity during an otherwise static chord:

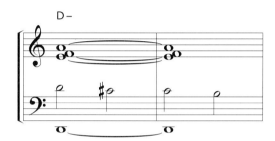

A line cliche:

- will move chromatically;

- always appears in the area of the chord where the 7th is normally structured (above the 5th);

- may demonstrate ascending or descending motion;

- will be found in any strata of the harmonies.

However, if the line cliche starts on the root of the chord, and is assigned to the bass voice, it must resolve, as in "My Funny Valentine" and "What Are You Doing the Rest of Your Life?."

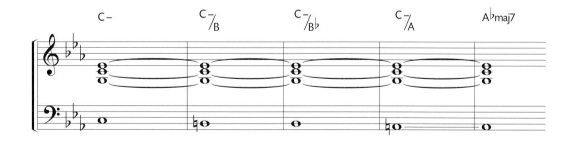

Chord scale treatment of line cliches is typically limited to the use of the triad pitches and the associated tensions with the line cliche pitch added. When ♯5 or ♭6 is encountered, only five notes are used.

D–

D– line cliche, pitch maj7 added

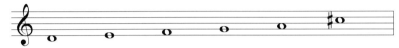

D– line cliche, pitch –7 added

D– line cliche, pitch 6 added

D–(♯5) or D–(♭6)

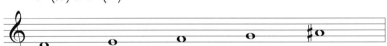

Line cliches are a favored arranging device and may be heard in major key on any of the diatonic minor chords. (The arrangement of "After the Lovin'" as done by Engelbert Humperdink is riddled with line cliches.) If the line cliche is appropriate, the minor chord may move to its related dominant 7th:

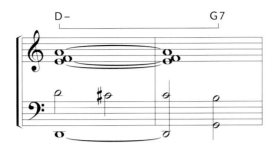

Line cliches will also be found in major key on the I and IV chords ("For Once In My Life;" "In the Wee Small Hours of the Morning").

MINOR TUNES TO ANALYZE

"Black Orpheus"

"Interplay"

"Hassan's Dream"

"Little Niles"

"What Are You Doing the Rest of Your Life"

"'Round Midnight"

"My Funny Valentine"

"Once I Loved (O Morro")

"Lament"

"You Don't Know What Love Is"

"Yesterdays"

"Alone Together"

"Minority"

"Summertime"

5
Blues

Blues has unique melody, harmony and form. Basic blues harmonies have, as their basis, early American Protestant church music. The primary cadences are *plagal* (subdominant) *cadences*. Typical of plagal cadence is the "A-men" following most hymns:

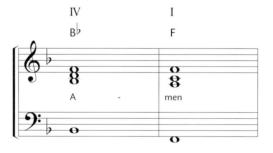

The primary chords of the fundamental blues are the I and IV triads.

The melodic pitches in the most basic blues is a minor pentatonic scale that is superimposed over the major key chords:

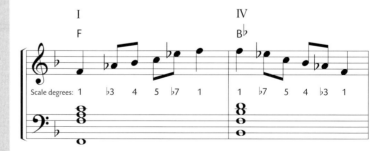

The important characteristics of the basic blues melodic pentatonic scale is the exclusion of half steps and the relationship of the ♭3 and ♭7 *blue notes* to the primary harmonic structures. The minor pentatonic (blues) scale and the major pentatonic scale have become valuable sources for jazz improvisation in blues as well as major and minor keys.

Blues form has its origin in the improvised lyrics. The lyrics of traditional blues are technically a rhymed couplet in iambic pentameter with the first line of the couplet repeated to allow additional time for preparation of the second line and the rhyme. Iambic pentameter is the rhythm of dotted eighth note – sixteenth note or dotted quarter note – eighth note repeated for five beats. If this pattern is observed for the couplet variation, the form of the basic *12-bar blues* can be seen:

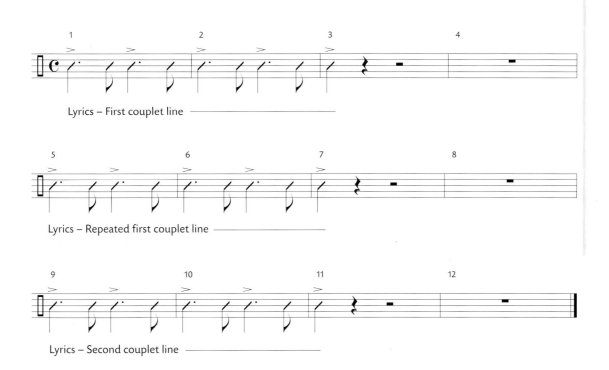

The primary blues seventh chords and tensions are derived from the blues melody pitches. The I7(♯9) and IV7(9) chord are examples of dominant chords without dominant function. They are tonic and subdominant functions respectively:

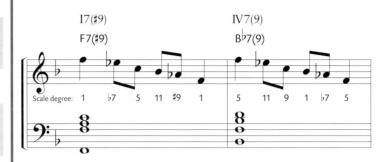

♭9 is usually not included as a tension on the tonic chord because it is not representative of the blues melodic scale; it would strongly suggest dominant function.

The V7 will appear in a basic blues. It can have dominant function or move diatonically to the IV7 chord:

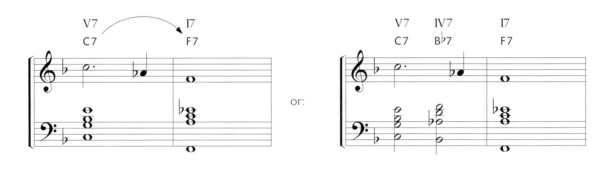

or:

Recall that the basic blues melodic scale does not contain half steps. With the use of dominant resolution, there is an inclusion of leading tone resolution by half step. This action ultimately resulted in the use of major key related functions. The basic melodic scale has also become more complex to include chromatic movement between scale degrees 4 and 5. The contemporary blue notes include ♭3, ♭7 and ♭5 (♯4):

The melodic and lyrical content of the blues is what creates the 12-bar blues form. The placement of the supporting harmonies within the form follows a logical sequence:

- The tonic chord is the most stressed.

- When the first line of the couplet is repeated, the use of different harmonies creates variety.

- Plagal cadence is primary; dominant cadence is secondary.

- The second line of the couplet contains the final cadence.

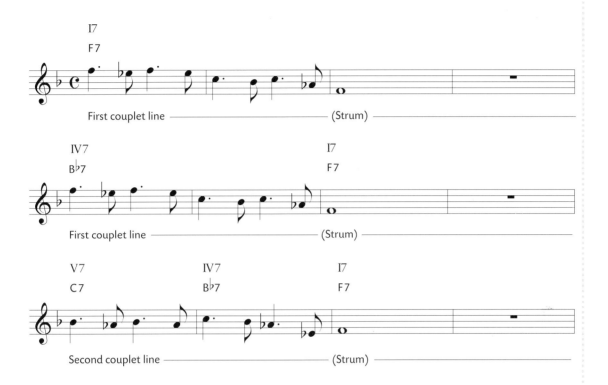

The lyrical content of a fundamental blues is within the first 2 measures of each 4-measure phrase. The remaining 2 measures begin with a cadence to the tonic chord. Because blues was most often performed by a soloist accompanying themselves, the last 2 measures of each phrase is know as the *strum*.

This recognizable blues progression contains some typical chords found in blues:

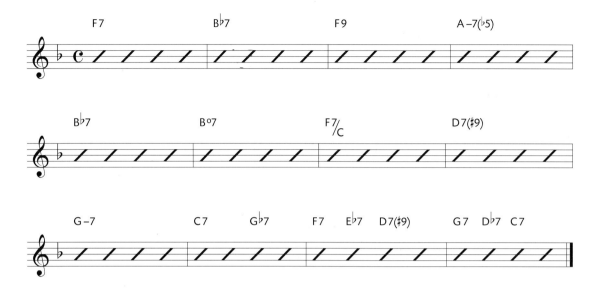

- The III–7(♭5) (A–7(♭5)) represents the upper structure of V9/IV (F9).
- The ♯IV°7 (B°7) is passing from the IV7 chord to the inverted tonic chord with chromatic root motion.
- There is secondary dominant function (V7/II) to a dominant cadence.
- The turnaround contains substitute and sequential dominants.

There is one important observation to note about the placement of the primary chords within the 12-bar blues form:

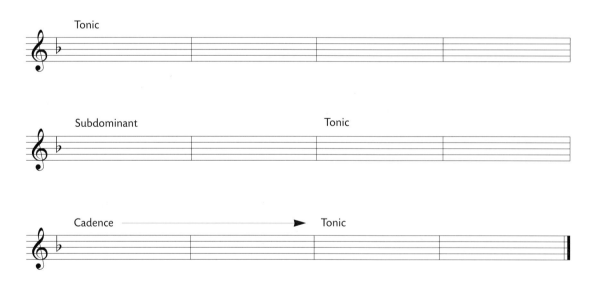

Any blues progression will follow this pattern. Variations to the pattern will occur in different ways:

- The progression may contain harmonic activity around the primary chord in each area, and/or

- there may be harmonic motion leading to the next primary chord.

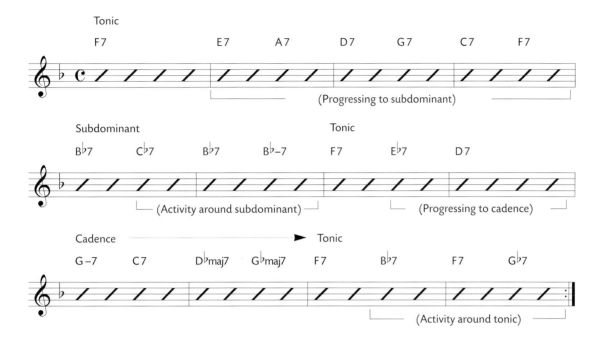

Here is a minor key blues variation:

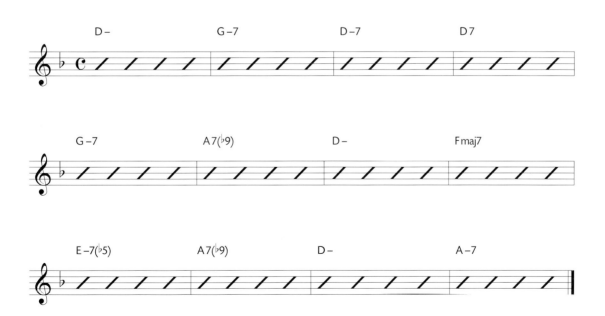

Here is a major key variation:

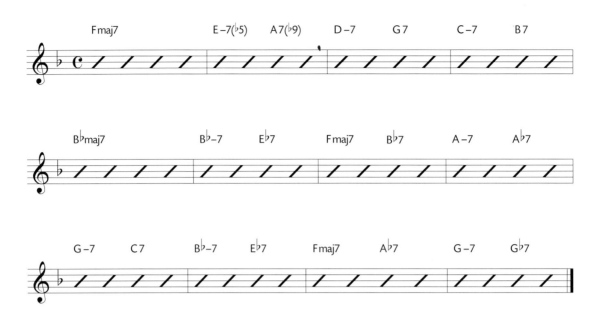

Major key or minor key or modal progressions may be inserted into the form. These alterations may or may not sound like blues though they are built around the blues form ("Bluesette" or "Blues For Alice" or the A sections of "Wave"). Some non-blues tunes use blues chords or blue notes for their color (the bridge of "Honeysuckle Rose" or "In a Mellow Tone" or "Mood Indigo"). Many popular tunes of the 1950s relied almost exclusively on blues influences.

Dependent upon context, the chord scales associated with blues can be varied. The non-chord tones for each chord can be derived from the blues scale or the major key or minor key function for the chord. The most common chord scale for the I7 chord (using pitches from blues and major key) is *Mixolydian ♯9*:

Other tonic chord scales can be fashioned using diatonic pitches from parallel tonalities:

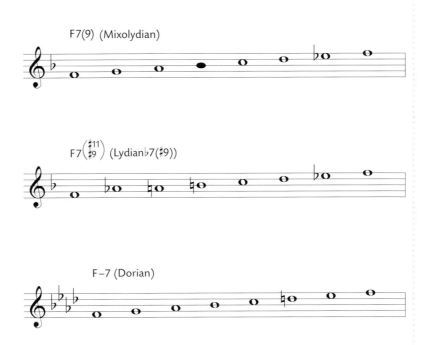

The IV7 chord most often uses a *Mixolydian* scale:

The V7 chord (borrowed from major key harmonies) is either a *Mixolydian* scale, or a *Mixolydian with alterations*, or an *altered* chord *scale*:

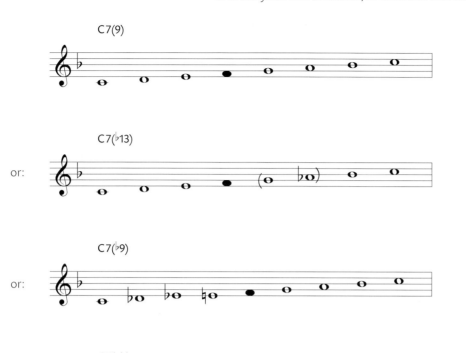

Other chords found in blues progressions are usually borrowed from major or minor key harmonies and therefore use their normal chord scales. V7/II, however, often takes a Mixolydian ♭9, ♯9, ♭13 chord scale. (A natural 9 would imply a major key, ♯9 (1 of the key) and ♭9 (♭7 of the key) are both blues melodic pitches.)

III–7(♭5), when acting as an approach chord to IV7, like most –7(♭5) chords, uses a Locrian chord scale (Locrian ♮9 is also possible since the ♮9 is a blue note):

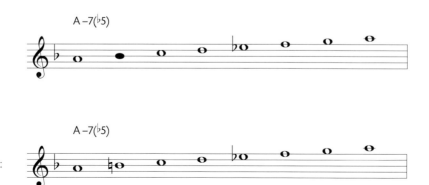

The chord scale for ♯IV°7 will be looked at in the chapter about diminished chords.

Natural 11 is not an available tension for dominant chords. However, in blues, it is *very common to find natural 11 as a stressed melodic pitch* on the primary I7, IV7, and V7 since in all these cases, ♮11 is a blues pitch.

Blues melody and blues harmonies = blues:

Because dominant chord structures are so typical of blues, in addition to the chord scales above, the symmetric dominant scale is worth investigating for potential usage.

The typical blues form is 12 measures; 24-bar blues is typical for triple meters. Variations to the 12-measure form include 8-bar blues and 16-bar blues. 8-bar blues can be achieved many ways, but one of the most common is the elimination of the subdominant cadence from measures 5 through 8, and the inclusion of a subdominant cadence in the first 4 measures:

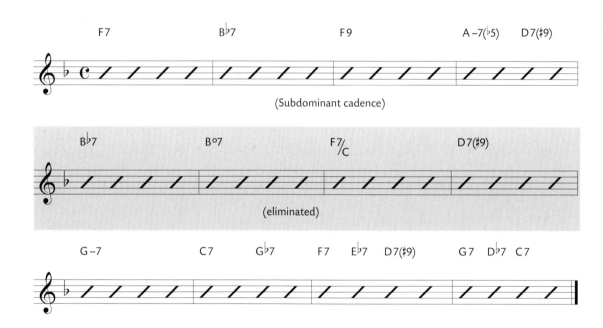

(Subdominant cadence)

(eliminated)

16-bar blues usually has an added 4 measures in the cadence area of a 12-bar
blues as an extension:

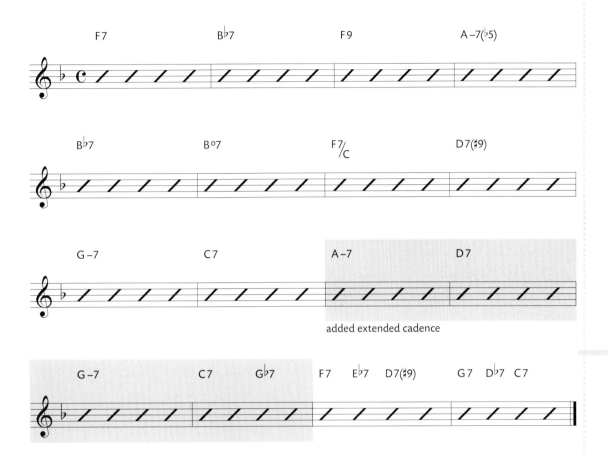

added extended cadence

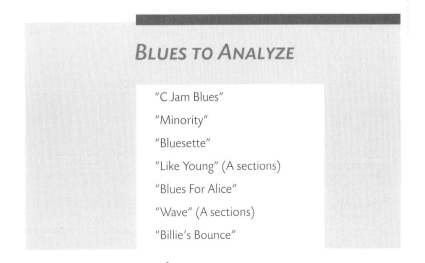

BLUES TO ANALYZE

"C Jam Blues"

"Minority"

"Bluesette"

"Like Young" (A sections)

"Blues For Alice"

"Wave" (A sections)

"Billie's Bounce"

6
Diminished
Seventh Chords

The first appearance of a diminished chord traces back to the 16th century. It was the result of individual melodic lines since harmony was not fully developed yet. The diminished triad built on the 7th scale degree and functioning as a dominant was the predecessor of the dominant seventh chord structure. To disguise the tritone between the root and diminished 5th it was used almost only in first inversion.

Some theorists believe that this chord was originally heard as consonant sound, which changed when the dominant seventh chord structure developed. The argument against it is that dissonant sounds in general are perceived as consonant sounds over time because we get used to them, but never the other way around.

However, this was the only diminished chord type (sometimes in root position) until around 1700. Since the time of J. S. Bach (18th century) also diminished seventh chords with primary and secondary dominant function had been employed. They are called leading tone chords, because the root is the tone leading to the root of the diatonic resolution chord. The diminished seventh chord represents the upper structure of the corresponding dominant chord.

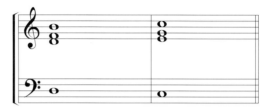

$G7(\flat 9) = B°7$

The structure of a diminished seventh chord is quite simple because of its symmetrical construction: three minor thirds superimposed. Because of the symmetry it may appear in various inversions and with different spellings, which confuses the analysis of diminished chords. This applies to classical music as well as to jazz and gets more complicated through simplified notation (readability) and wrong notation (lead sheets).

Although the diminished seventh chord has diatonic origin (harmonic minor), its application in the 18th and 19th century as a nondiatonic structure with diatonic function was important for the development of chromaticism and the extension of tonality. This is related to the symmetrical structure of diminished chords.

As mentioned already, in traditional music diminished seventh chords appear mostly functioning as **primary and secondary dominants**. They may precede any diatonic chord except VII–7(♭5). The root of the diminished seventh chord is the leading tone to the root of the diatonic resolution chord (leading tone chords). Because of the symmetrical structure each note may be interpreted as a new root which gives a number of possibilities for modulation. In jazz the re-interpretation of diminished seventh chords for modulation is rare.

In Western art music **nondominant diminished seventh chords** most often function as embellishment. They have a common tone root with, most often, I or V. They move from the diatonic chord and back to the same chord. (They are also known as common tone or auxiliary diminished chords):

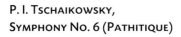

P. I. TSCHAIKOWSKY,
SYMPHONY NO. 6 (PATHITIQUE)

Another category of diminished seventh chords is related to the previous one. Also nondominant, they have more than one tone – except the root – in common with the diatonic resolution chord. They appear commonly in jazz (♭VIo7 and ♭IIIo7) and will be discussed in more detail. In classical music the ♭VIo7 chord is an exception, because it also appears as a dominant functioning inversion of VIIo7:

L. V. BEETHOVEN, OP. 79

TYPICAL DIMINISHED PATTERNS

Passing diminished 7th chords have long been used as a means of dealing with parallel voice leading, the result of diatonic movement between adjacent chords. In contemporary usage, the diminished chord may be either a *passing* diminished (if the preparatory chord is present) or an *approaching* diminished. The most typical patterns are:

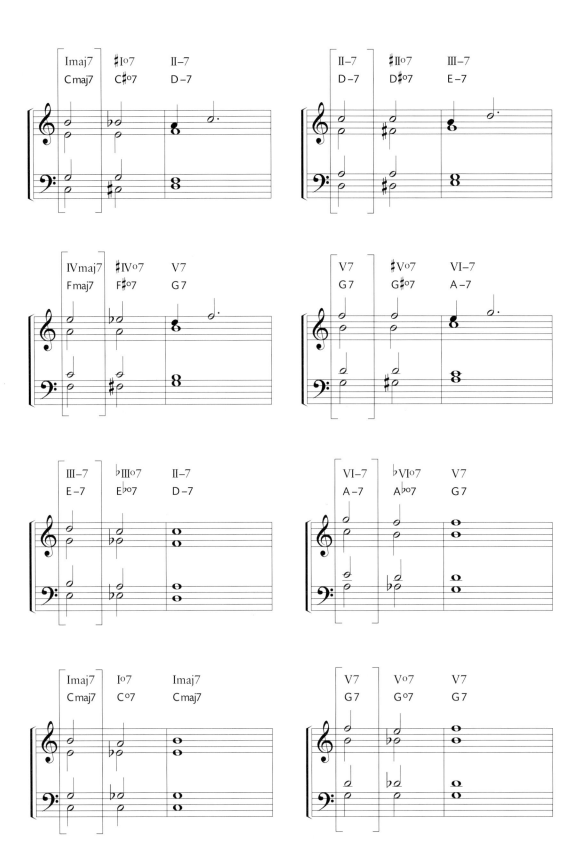

These diatonic functioning diminished 7th chords can be categorized as either:

- *ascending* to the diatonic chord a half step higher, or
- *descending* to the diatonic chord a half step lower, or
- an *auxiliary* of the tonic or dominant chord (with no root movement).

The above patterns are the most common. However, some of the above chords are used less frequently than in the recent past, and rare examples of IV°7 and ♭V°7 exist. In addition to the normal diatonic resolutions, commonly found alternate resolutions are:

♯I°7 has an expected resolution to the II–7 chord. It has an alternate resolution to the related dominant of II–7: V7 with its 5th in the bass:

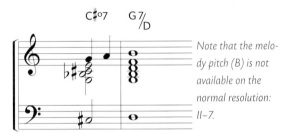

Note that the melody pitch (B) is not available on the normal resolution: II–7.

♯II°7 has an expected resolution to the tonic III–7 chord. It has an alternate resolution to the tonic I chord with its 3rd in the bass:

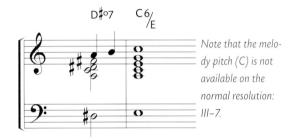

Note that the melody pitch (C) is not available on the normal resolution: III–7.

♯IV°7 has an expected resolution to the primary dominant. It has an alternate resolution to the tonic I chord with its 5th in the bass:

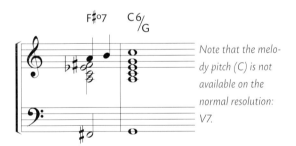

Note that the melody pitch (C) is not available on the normal resolution: V7.

♯V°7 has an expected resolution to VI–7. It has an alternate resolution to the secondary dominant chord built on the same root: V7/II:

♭III°7 has an expected resolution to the II–7 chord. It has an alternate resolution to the II–7's related V7 with its 5th in the bass:

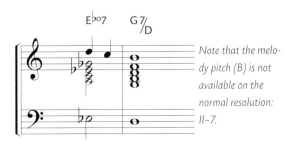

Note that the melody pitch (B) is not available on the normal resolution: II–7.

♭VI°7 has an expected resolution to V7. It has an alternate resolution to I with its 5th in the bass:

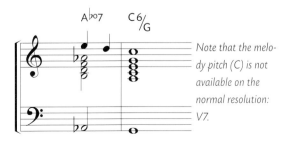

Note that the melody pitch (C) is not available on the normal resolution: V7.

The auxiliary diminished chords do not have alternative resolutions. Most of the alternate resolutions are inversions in order for the diminished chord's root to resolve appropriately. However, sometimes the alternate chord appears in root position. Also, because all diminished 7th chords are symmetrically built in minor 3rds, many lead sheets contain an incorrect root name for a correct sounding diminished chord.

DIMINISHED CHORD SCALES

A diminished 7th chord contains 2 tritones, so there is a possibility of these chords having dominant function. With regard to the ascending diminished chords, the tritone of the secondary dominant of the target chord is present. (In traditional usage, the ascending diminished 7ths are referred to as secondary dominant chords in first inversion.) However, the descending and auxiliary diminished *do not* contain the secondary dominant's tritone, therefore, the descending and auxiliary diminished are derived from *chromatic resolution* as opposed to dominant resolution. This is an important fact with regard to the chord scale choices (dominant versus nondominant). The important characteristics of diminished chords are:

- They have a diatonic resolution and function.
- Each is built symmetrically.
- They are not diatonic structures.
- Two tritones are present.
- The chord scales will contain 8 notes (4 chord tones and 4 nonchord tones).

Refer to the chord scales introduced in the beginning chapter *Harmonic Structures*. The symmetric diminished scale was symmetric step-half step:

C°7 = symmetric diminished

No avoid notes–a great scale! But on closer examination, there is a problem with the symmetric diminished scale and the characteristics of the diminished 7th chords mentioned above. These chords have *diatonic function*, hence, the tensions should be *diatonic*. If the tensions of the above symmetric diminished chord scale (the D, F, A♭, and B♮) are arranged into a key signature, there is no recognizable key:

Result–the symmetric diminished chord scale is an appropriate scale for use when the diminished 7th chord is *not* functioning diatonically. (Recall that the half step–whole step symmetric scale is *symmetric dominant*, not a diminished chord scale.)

For the diatonic functioning diminished chords, a more appropriate chord scale must rely on the diatonic functioning *secondary dominant chords* which contain the necessary 8 notes. These are the Mixolydian chord scales with ♭9 and ♯9.

Because the ascending diminished chords are derived from the *secondary dominant of the target diatonic chord of resolution*, that secondary dominant chord scale is the choice for the diminished chord scale:

Note that the chord scales for these ascending diminished chords:

- are displacements of the secondary dominant chord scale (starting on the 3rd; recall *leading tone root* on page 110),
- all contain 8 pitches,
- have tensions and avoid notes which are diatonic,
- contain avoid notes that represent 11 and ♭13 of the secondary dominant except,
- the chord scale for an inverted V7(♭9) of V, which is the same as ♯IV°7, contains an additional tension.

These are the chord scales for the ascending diminished 7th chords, for each meets the necessary criteria.

The chord scale for each of the nondominant derived diminished chords will use one of the same scales but it will not have dominant function with regard to the target diatonic chord because these descending and auxiliary diminished chords are not derived from dominant function. The scale of choice is based on the enharmonic similarities between the ascending diminished chords and the chromatically derived diminished chord because the key remains unchanged. (Refer to the scales on the previous page.)

♯I°7 and V°7 contain the same enharmonic chord tones:

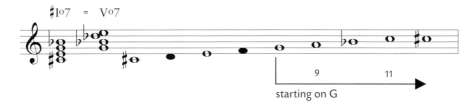

♯V°7 and ♭VI°7 are enharmonically the same:

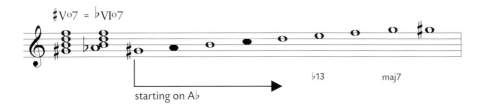

I°7 and ♭III°7 are enharmonically equivalent to ♯II°7:

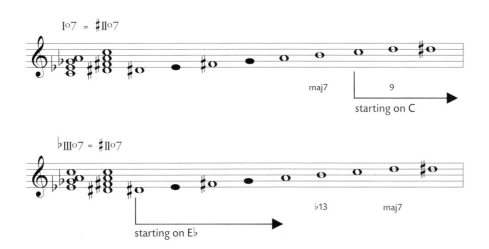

For demonstration purposes, the above scales begin with the root of the related enharmonic chord. The starting pitch of the scale is the root of the diminished chord. The tension numbers represent those for the enharmonic diminished chord. There are two chord scales usable for the ♯IV°7 chord; V7(♭9) of V because of dominant derivation (see the previous ascending diminished scales) and V7(♭9) of III because it is enharmonically the same as ♯II°7:

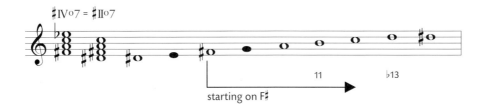

Similarly, it is possible to use the dominant functioning chord scale for #IV°7, which contains an additional tension, for the enharmonically similar #II°7, bIII°7, and I°7 chords (V7(b9, #9) of V). The choice of chord scale for these diminished chords must take into consideration the most appropriate tensions. V7(b9, #9) of V contains a nondiatonic tension while V7(b9, #9) of III contains all diatonic tensions and one represents the tonic of the key. From a linear (playing) viewpoint, both scales are usable. From a harmonic (chordal) viewpoint, the secondary dominant of III tends to sound best.

Note that the tensions for the diminished 7th chords are unusually numbered because the diminished chord is symmetrically structured. 9, 11, b13 are common tensions, maj7 is usually considered a chord tone, but here it is a tension.

Jazz musicians have had a fondness for reharmonization. It appeals to our artistic nature. Diminished 7th chords are particularly ripe for reharmonization because of their nonspecific demand for diatonic resolution. While in the '20s and '30s diminished chords were common, they have been reharmonized when Bebop developed ('40s). The *ascending* diminished 7th chords can be reharmonized by substituting the secondary dominant of the diatonic target chord. Including the related II–7(b5) gives a more active and more interesting harmony which also allows for deceptive dominant resolution. *The melody must allow for any of these chord substitutions*:

REHARMONIZATION OF DIMINISHED CHORDS

Original with diminished chords:

Reharmonization:

When a diminished chord resolves to an inverted alternate resolution target chord (Cmaj7 in the 3rd measure above), the reharmonization chord will move to a target in root position. Note that the reharmonization is made more complete by including the related II–7(♭5) of the dominant chord. This is done to imply the sound of the original diminished 7th by using a *half diminished* chord followed by a *full diminished* as the upper structure within the dominant:

The reharmonizations for the *chromatically* derived diminished chords will all have nondominant, or deceptive, resolutions:

Original with diminished chords:

Reharmonization:

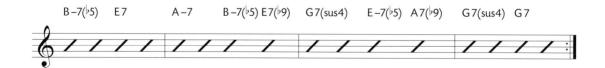

Some diminished chords reharmonize better than others. There are recent tunes which have been composed with the reharmonizations for the diminished chords built in as the original changes (measures 3 and 4 of "Meditation" in lieu of I°7). Older standard tunes have used the reharmonizations more often than the original diminished chords (the first 2 measures of "Stella by Starlight" in lieu of the original ♭III°7).

♯IV−7(♭5) is included here because it is closely related to diminished 7th chords in structure and function. It can be heard as sometimes functioning like a half diminished chord. ♯IV−7(♭5) sounds like a modal interchange chord from Lydian:

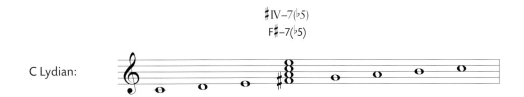

♯IV−7(♭5) is very often preceded by root motion down a half step from the V7 chord, and as such is a common deceptive resolution for the dominant chord of the key:

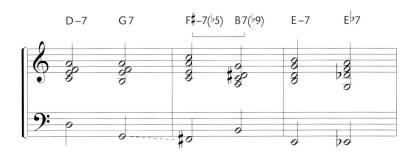

Movement from the ♯IV–7(♭5) chord is either

- (as above) to V7(♭9) of III (its related secondary dominant chord), or

- down or up a half step to a form of IV or V or inverted I over its 5th (similar to diminished 7th chord motion). We have grown very accustomed to hearing ♯IV–7(♭5) moving to a IV–7 or IV–6 chord with eventual resolution back to tonic:

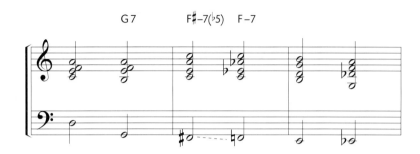

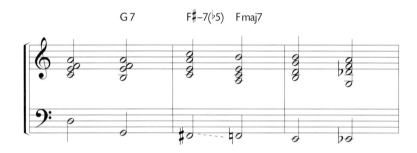

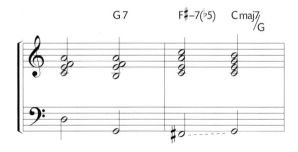

♯IV–7(♭5) has diatonic function and uses a diatonically oriented Locrian chord scale. Locrian (♮9) is also a potential chord scale when movement is expected to a IV– chord. (♮9 represents the –3rd of the IV– chord):

F♯ Locrian:

F♯ Locrian ♮9:

The VIIº7 is most often a modal interchange chord from harmonic minor and can function as a passing or approaching diminished chord. As a diatonic chord, it can move either to the I chord or any other chord with diatonic function as in Jobim's "How Insensitive." The chord scale for VIIº7 is a displacement of harmonic minor (starting on the 7th degree) or V7(Mixolydian ♭9, ♯9, ♭13) starting on the 3rd (leading tone root). Both chord scales indicate a dominant quality for the VIIº7 chord:

VIIº7

TUNES TO ANALYZE WITH DIMINISHED 7TH CHORDS AND ♯IV–7(♭5)

"How Insensitive"

"Liza"

"The Song Is You"

"I Remember Clifford"

"Wave"

7

Dominant Chords
with
Special Functions

All secondary dominants and their substitute secondary dominants have potential for other special functions. A review of the Blues chapter will show chords which function as tonic and subdominant blues sounds; the I7 and IV7 chords. Although both chords are dominant structures, they *do not* have dominant function. To demonstrate the different functions for the same chord, listen to a blues progression which begins on the I7 and contains a V7/IV at the end of the 4th measure:

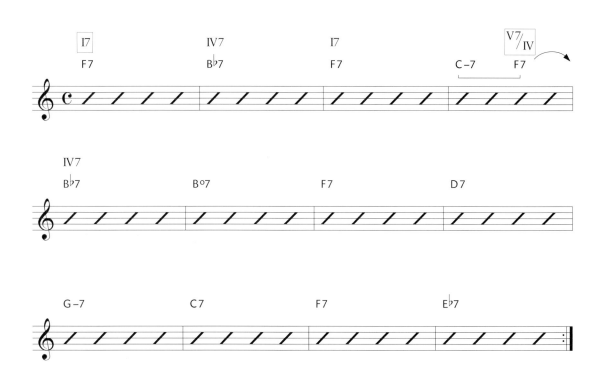

The I7 tonic chord and IV7 subdominant chord are not uncommon in progressions other than blues ("I'm All Smiles," "Sophisticated Lady," "Moon River," "On a Clear Day," "Tenderly").

Similarly, other chords with dominant structure, but nondominant function, are related to the blues by having *blue note roots*. ♭VII7, most often a modal interchange/subdominant minor chord, is built on a blue note, as is ♭V7 and ♭III7. These chords may sound and function as diatonic blues chords instead of their potential functions as subV of II, IV, and VI respectively. The ♭V7 and ♭III7 are unusual, but when any of the blues rooted dominant chords progress, they usually cadence to tonic or move by diatonic blues scale step:

(Indeed, in the above progression, even the V7 may be looked upon as having a special function other than as the primary dominant.) In such situations, the chord scale for each chord may be either Lydian ♭7 (describing motion *other than* down a perfect 5th) or any form of Mixolydian (describing expectation for *resolution* down a perfect 5th), or symmetric dominant, depending on the choice of the player/writer and circumstances. Stylistic considerations can enter into the picture. For example, many Motown tunes from the '60s and '70s use chords which appear to be blues based, but in fact originate from parallel guitar barre chord voicings ("Knock on Wood," "Proud Mary," "Sittin' on the Dock of the Bay," etc.). Because the chords are parallel structures (without dominant function), each dominant chord will use the same chord scale as that of its parallel neighbor (usually Mixolydian). ♭V7 is most often found as a cadence chord to tonic ("The Island" – nonblues context, "Good-bye Pork Pie Hat" – blues):

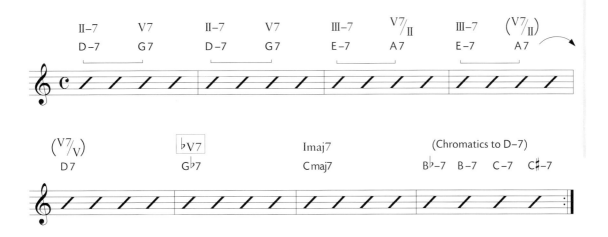

The above progression may be viewed as "some original" changes for the A sections of the standard "Satin Doll."

♭VI7 has been seen before as a modal interchange chord from the minor key. Some musicians argue that it is more closely related to a blues function. Either perspective results in a chord whose function, as a cadential chord to tonic, uses a Lydian ♭7 chord scale. "Bye Bye Blues" will demonstrate this:

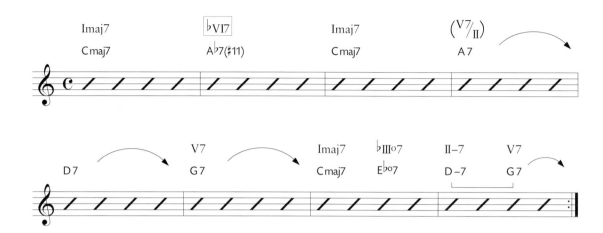

SPECIAL FUNCTIONS FOR SECONDARY DOMINANTS

All secondary dominant chords will be found having functions other than the norm. V7/IV occurs as I7; V7/II occurs as VI7; V7/III occurs as VII7; V7/V occurs as II7; V7/VI occurs as III7.

VI7 is found in situations where its expectation is to resolve deceptively as V7/II to V7/V or an inverted V7/V. This would be the beginning of a logical progression back to tonic:

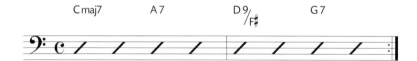

Instead of a final dominant cadence, a subdominant minor cadence to tonic might occur with VI7 moving to either IV(−) or ♯IV−7(♭5):

The chord tones of the ♯IV−7(♭5) above are the upper notes of the V9/V chord.

In rarer instances, VI7 may cadence directly to tonic as in some rock tunes from the '50s or the last phrase of "You Must Have Been a Beautiful Baby:"

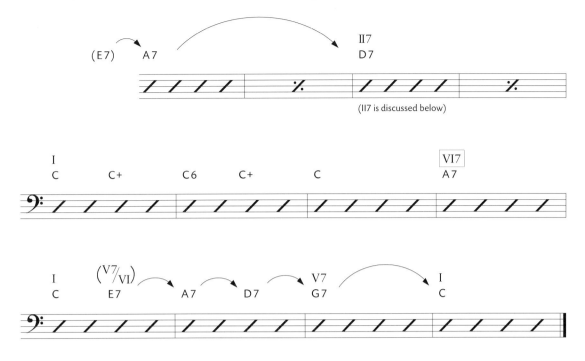

(II7 is discussed below)

The chord scale for VI7 is most often a form of Mixolydian.

VII7 can be heard in circumstances where its normal function as V7/III is superceded by its possibility to cadence to a stronger tonic chord:

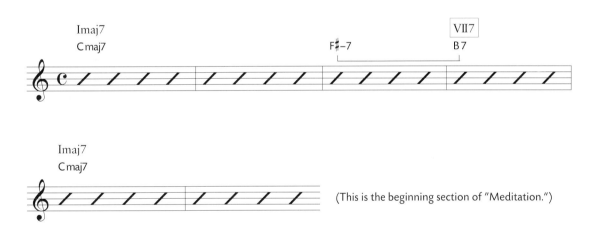

(This is the beginning section of "Meditation.")

VII7 occurs in cadential resolutions to tonic (usually due to harmonic rhythm). Reviewing the information about reharmonization of diminished chords will show that VII7 can move to I as the reharmonization for I°7 or it can move to II–7 or IV as the reharmonization for ♭III°7 ("Summer Samba"). The chord scale choices for VII7 are any form of Mixolydian, altered, Lydian ♭7, or symmetric dominant. (Listen to the first four measures of "Meditation" using any form of dominant scale for the VII7 chord.)

II7 (most often V7/V) is also found in cadential resolutions to tonic, usually due to harmonic rhythm:

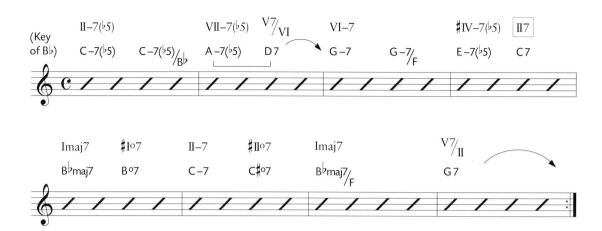

Observe the similarities existing between the II7 and the ♯IV–7(♭5) in the above tune (Quincy Jones' "Stockholm Sweetnin'"). Both (along with ♭VI7) contain the same tritone and are often found substituting for each other.

In the relative minor key, the II7 chord of the relative major key has a very close relationship with the tonic minor chord, and therefore may appear as the last chord in the relative minor section of a progression which returns to the relative major key:

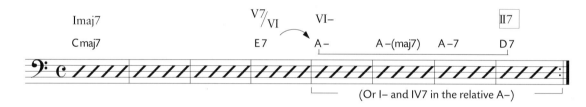

The chord scale for II7 is a choice between Lydian ♭7 and, more commonly, any form of Mixolydian.

The movement of VII7 up a half step to Imaj7 is mimicked by movement of III7 up a half step to IVmaj7. III7 to IV will occur in place of V7/IV resolving to IV: III7 has already been seen as a dominant chord starting a sequential dominant series. Reference to blues ("Wave" if you look at it), will reveal that III7 may occur following a V7/I chord. This is a situation where the III7 is a nondominant function, substituting for tonic. (Also see measure 3 of "The Dolphin.")

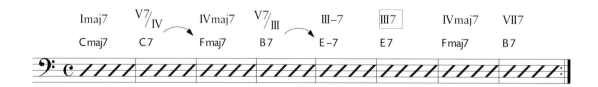

III7 may also have its origins in deceptive resolution of the primary V7 (E7) in the relative minor (A–), deceptively resolving to ♭VImaj7 (Fmaj7) but without a concluding tonic minor cadence. Any dominant chord scale will work for III7.

To summarize the nondominant functions of dominant structured chords:

nondominant function	secondary dominant function	motion to
I7	V7/IV	n/a
II7	V7/V	I or IV
♭III7	subV7/II	I or IV
III7	V7/VI	IV
IV7	subV7/III*	I or III–
♭V7	subV7/IV	I or V
♭VI7	subV7/V	I
VI7	V7/II	♯IV–7(♭5) or IV(–) or I
♭VII7	subV7/VI*	any tonic function
VII7	V7/III	I or II– or IV

* The nondominant function of these two chords is much more common than their secondary substitute dominant function.

The choice of chord scale for any of the special functioning dominant chords is partially governed by the diatonic; either major, minor, or blues. Another factor for choice is the expectation for possible cadence, and therefore, root motion (expectation versus actual). The symmetric dominant chord scale is particularly suited for special function dominants because it contains all the dominant scales characteristics.

If the chord of question sounds like a secondary or substitute secondary dominant, the secondary dominant analysis holds sway, and hence, the secondary dominant chord scale. If the same chord is truly performing a special function, the choice of chord scale will communicate a special function to the listener.

TUNES TO ANALYZE FOR SPECIAL FUNCTION DOMINANTS

"I'm All Smiles"

"Sophisticated Lady"

"Moon River"

"The Island"

"Good-bye Pork Pie Hat"

"You Must Have Been a Beautiful Baby"

"Stockholm Sweetnin'"

"Meditation"

"I Remember Clifford"

"Someday My Prince Will Come"

"Speak Low"

"Spring Can Really Hang You Up The Most"

"Out of Nowhere"

"This Can't Be Love"

"On a Clear Day"

"Summer Samba"

8

Modal Interchange

PARALLEL DIATONIC KEYS

The borrowing of chords from parallel tonalities has already been explored in the chapter dealing with *minor key harmony* and was limited to the use of diatonic chords from the common minor tonalities. To review: one form of modal interchange involves the use of diatonic chords from any of the minor keys (natural, harmonic, melodic, dorian minor) in a free mixture, resulting in a totally minor progression (the first 4 measures of "Lament"):

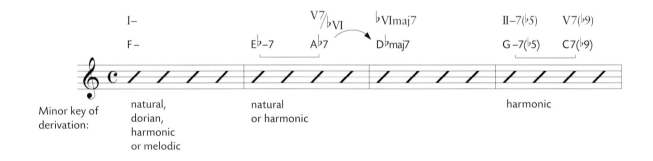

II–7(♭5) V7(♭9) is frequently used as a harmonic minor color in a major key progression ("You Go To My Head"):

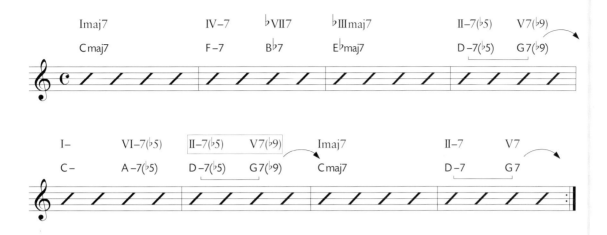

The other common form of modal interchange is borrowing natural minor chords for use in the parallel major key. The modal interchange chords which result can be categorized as functioning as either tonic minor sounds (TM) or subdominant minor chords (SDM):

I–7	II–7(♭5)	♭IIImaj7	IV–7	V–7	♭VImaj7	♭VII7	I–7
TM	SDM	TM	SDM	TM	SDM	SDM	TM
Dor.	Loc.	Lyd.	Dor.	Dor.	Lyd.	Lyd.♭7	Dor.

The chord scales for the natural minor (aeolian) chords were developed using a combination of diatonic choices from the parallel major and minor keys. Because these chords are so prevalent in contemporary music, we have become accustomed to the scales as previously described. However, in a more pure sense, a less complicated approach would be to use only *diatonic* pitches from the mode of interchange. Although the concept of borrowing not only chords but chord scale choices would appear to be a theoretical step backwards, the resulting change of "color" through the use of seldom used scales is worthy of investigation:

C–7	D–7(♭5)	E♭maj7	F–7	G–7	A♭maj7	B♭7	C–7
Aeol.	Loc.	Ion.	Dor.	Phry.	Lyd.	Mixo.	Aeol.

COMMON
INTERCHANGE CHORDS

Other modes of interchange can be found, as well as the possibility of experimentation with more esoteric scale choices. In addition to Aeolian, the other diatonic modes are the most likely candidates for producing usable chords and chord scales.

Lydian modal interchange:

The most often used chord from Lydian is the ♯IV–7(♭5) (Locrian chord scale). A lesser used chord is the VII–7 (Phrygian chord scale) ("Promises, Promises"). Using VII–7 as a cadential chord to tonic Imaj will produce a pure Lydian sound. The other chords for use in major key are II7 (Mixolydian chord scale) (which is usually V7/V or as described in the previous chapter as a secondary dominant with special function) and the obscure Vmaj7 (the I chord of the relative major scale). However, more common to Lydian modal interchange is the use of the diatonic chord scale in the parallel major. The I Lydian chord is very common – the use of III–9 (Aeolian) is also common:

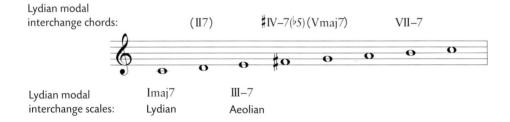

Lydian modal interchange scales:		
Imaj7	III–7	
Lydian	Aeolian	

(Chords/scales in parentheses are either very obscure or more commonly derived from another function or parallel modal source.)

A common Lydian alternative is the II chord superimposed above the tonic note ("Dolphin Dance"); the resulting chord will be looked at later as a tonic hybrid chord:

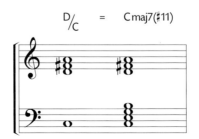

Mixolydian modal interchange:

II–7(♭5) (Locrian chord scale) and ♭VIImaj7 (Lydian chord scale) are Mixolydian modal interchange chords/scales ("Why Did I Choose You?," "Lush Life"):

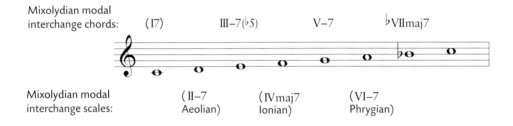

Of the chords generated by the Mixolydian mode, the I7 is most often a blues sound, as is the Mixolydian scale associated with the I7. The V–7 (Dorian chord scale) chord is found in cadences to tonic I ("Dreamsville," "Never Can Say Good-bye," "Old Devil Moon"). With the V–7 structured over the tonic note of the key, a I7(sus4) results as an alternate structure ("Viola" and "Johnny One Note"):

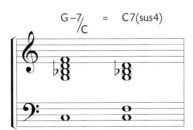

Dorian modal interchange:

The modal interchange interest this mode has to offer is the VI–7(♭5) (Locrian chord scale) chord, the IV7 (Mixolydian chord scale) chord (which is closely related to blues), and the possible use of the diatonic chord scales:

Dorian modal
interchange chords:

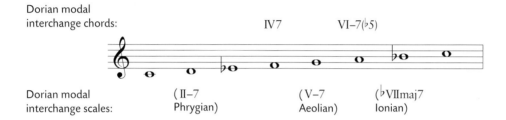

Dorian modal
interchange scales:

Phrygian modal interchange:

C–7   D♭maj7   E♭7   F–7   G–7(♭5)   A♭maj7   B♭–7   C–7

Phrygian modal interchange produces some rarely used but interesting chords/scales. The Phrygian I–7 chord makes for an unusual color choice ("Interplay"). The ♭IImaj7 (Lydian chord scale) chord derived from this mode was discussed in the chapter on minor keys. ♭III7 is closely related to blues harmonies; the IV–7 and ♭VImaj7 to minor key harmonies. V–7(♭5) (Locrian chord scale) is very rare. The ♭VII–7 (Dorian chord scale) chord has use as a cadential alternative for ♭IImaj7 ("Temptation," "Little B's Poem") :

Phrygian modal
interchange chords: ♭IImaj7 (♭III7)   (V–7(♭5))   (♭VII–7)

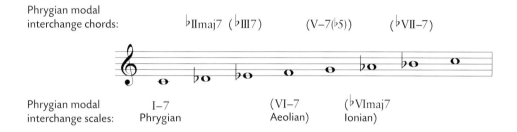

Phrygian modal   I–7   (VI–7   (♭VImaj7
interchange scales: Phrygian   Aeolian)   Ionian)

Locrian modal interchange:

C –7(♭5) D♭maj7 E♭–7 F –7 G♭maj7 A♭7 B♭–7 C –7(♭5)

The tonic I–7(♭5) (Locrian chord scale) is very unusual, but does exist ("Tones For Joan's Bones," "I Will Say Good-bye"). ♭IImaj7, IV–7, and ♭VII–7 are generally not derived from this mode. ♭Vmaj7 (Lydian chord scale) (the music of Chick Corea and Steely Dan), and ♭III–7 (Phrygian chord scale) ("Forestflower" and as a chromatic passing chord between II–7 and III–7) are potential cadence chords to tonic major. ♭VI7 (Mixolydian chord scale) ("Good-bye Pork Pie Hat" and "Armageddon") is found occasionally:

Locrian modal
interchange chords: (I–7(♭5))   (♭III–7)   ♭Vmaj7

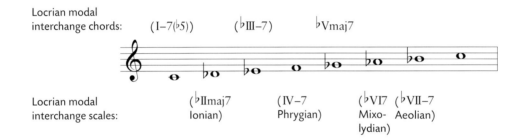

Locrian modal   (♭IImaj7)   (IV–7)   (♭VI7   (♭VII–7
interchange scales: Ionian)   Phrygian)   Mixo-   Aeolian)
                                                          lydian)

A very common modal interchange of *minor to major* occurs by deceptive resolution of dominants: V7/I–, V7/II–, V7/III–, V7/VI–. The root of the expected resolution chord becomes the tonic of the new key. A continuation of "Lament" can demonstrate:

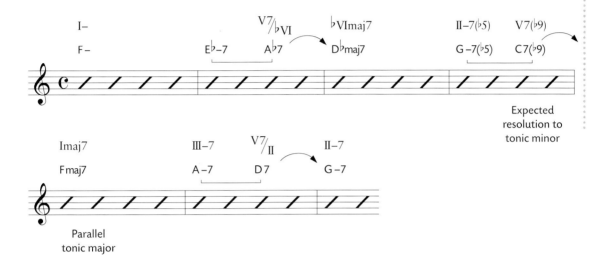

A complete discussion of advanced modal theory is beyond the scope of this text – there is an examination of basic modal harmonies later. However, in addition to the diatonic modes, other common, and uncommon modes for possible interchange chords and scales deserve to be examined by interested writers and players: modes of harmonic minor, modes of melodic minor, Spanish Phrygian, as well as innumerable synthetic modes and their displacements.

TUNES TO ANALYZE FOR MODAL INTERCHANGE CHORDS

"Promises, Promises"

"Dindi"

"Dolphin Dance"

"Lush Life"

"Look to the Sky"

"I Love You"

"Dreamsville"

"Never Can Say Good-bye"

"Interplay"

"Old Devil Moon"

9

Voicing Specific Chord Symbols and Structures

SLASH CHORDS

Contemporary music is producing an ever increasing number of examples of progressions with stylistically specific chord voicings. Without these inversions, hybrids, and polychords, progressions will tend to sound generic and common place. It is important to be able to recognize, and therefore assign an appropriate chord scale to what may appear as an unrecognizable chord symbol.

The chord symbols used in the following are not yet totally universal. A diagonal slash (/) will be used to indicate a complete upper structure (triad or 7th chord) with an independent root or an inverted chord:

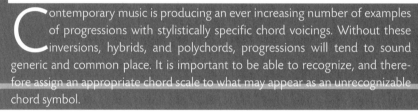

A horizontal line (–) will be used to indicate a complete upper structure supported by a complete lower structure (either triads or 7th chords):

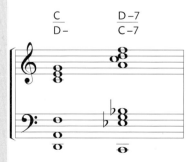

Inverted chords are frequently found in today's music. An *inversion* is a chord that is not in root position. Either the 3rd, 5th, or 7th is in the bass. (Some chords which appear to be inversions will be heard as hybrids.) Generally, inversions fit into a few categories:

Recall that there are inverted alternate *resolutions for passing diminished chords* in order for the root of the diminished to move chromatically as in "Liza."

The alternative resolution chords involved with passing diminished chord progressions are the inverted I and V chords. The inverted chords use the diatonic chord scale. However, the voicing almost always contains only chord tones and occasionally little tension. The use of too many available tensions obscures the sound of the chord, and in fact may produce an unwanted sound of another chord.

Another common inversion is seen in situations where the 3rd is in the bass of a dominant chord (functioning as the leading tone of the target chord of resolution):

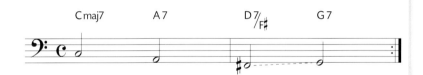

Descending bass lines create inversions. A chord progression can be given new life through this technique. Bill Evans recorded "Waltz for Debby" without inversions and with a descending bass line that ultimately resolved with a leading tone to the target IV chord in root position:

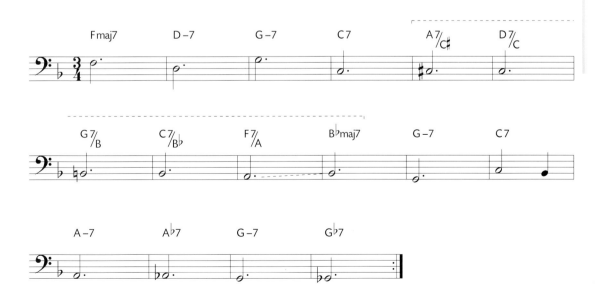

<table>
<tr><td>

UPPER STRUCTURE TRIADS

</td><td>

Upper structure triads are a voicing technique that are worthy of mention here because they have a direct relationship to hybrids. *An upper structure triad contains a high degree of tension from the chord scale and is supported by the chord sound:*

</td></tr>
</table>

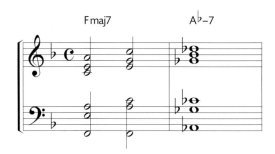

The method of construction is straight forward. Determine the appropriate *chord scale*; using the melody pitch as one note of a triad, construct a *major or minor triad* with tensions; *support the triad* with the chord sound. (For more information about voicing techniques, see the "Introduction to Arranging" chapter.):

Ab Dorian:

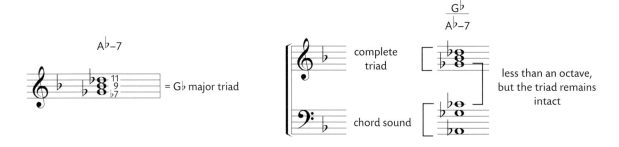

The spacing within the voicing is critical. The upper and lower structures must each be independently identifiable, but both must sound as a complete entity.

A hybrid chord will contain an upper structure triad (sometimes a 7th chord) supported by an independent root. In its simplest form, a *hybrid* may be viewed as an upper structure triad without the chord sound support. Most often, when combined, the four or five notes of a hybrid will *not* equal a 7th chord:

$$\frac{G\flat}{A\flat} \qquad \frac{Fmaj7}{G} \qquad \frac{E}{G} \qquad \frac{B-}{C} \qquad \frac{G-7}{A\flat} \qquad \frac{D\flat}{G} \qquad \frac{A\flat}{D\flat} \qquad \frac{G}{A\flat}$$

One exception to the above is the hybrid discussed previously as a Lydian modal interchange scale for the I chord. The same hybrid may be used for any Lydian or Lydian♭7 chord scale. Dominant 7th (sus4) chords are commonly expressed as hybrids:

Lydian or Lydian♭7		V7(sus4)	V7(sus4)	V7(sus4)	V7(sus4)	V7(sus4)
$\frac{D}{C}$	(not D7 inverted)	$\frac{F}{G}$	$\frac{F6}{G}$	$\frac{Fmaj7}{G}$	$\frac{D-}{G}$	$\frac{D-7}{G}$

Hybrids are *ambiguous* because they lack complete chord sound. Context is what defines to the listener the true function of the chord:

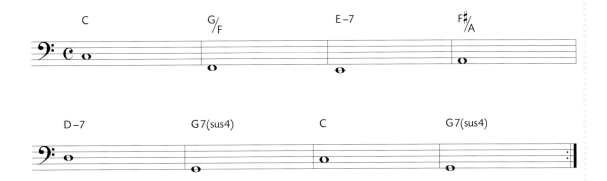

Stevie Wonder's "You Are the Sunshine of My Life" contains an inversion with a descending root as well as a hybrid. An understanding of the construction method for hybrids will, in reverse fashion, explain the actual function for a hybrid. The first step in the process is to determine the chord scale choice; the root of the chord is the support; a triad is built using the melody pitch and available notes from the chord scale, except the 3rd is avoided. This exclusion of the 3rd is what makes the sound ambiguous. (The 3rd is available for dominant chords because the lack of a 7th is enough to create ambiguity.) Spacing of the hybrid is not as critical as with upper structure triads:

A symmetric dominant:

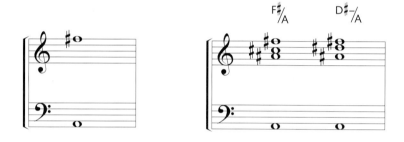

Avoided notes are assessed on an individual basis. In the above dominant scale, the ♯9 has been avoided because it will sound like a minor 3rd.

There may be many chord scale choices for a hybrid. The F♯/A in the above tune is either a Mixolydian(♭9) or a symmetric dominant. Either scale, in the context of this progression, can be used for a V7/II chord:

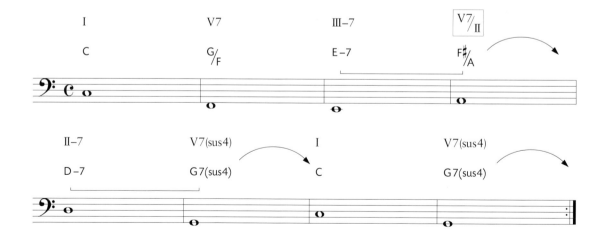

olychords are also related to upper structure triads. A *polychord* is a structure which has two complete chords.

P olychords are also related to upper structure triads. A *polychord* is a structure which has two complete chords.

P olychords are also related to upper structure triads. A *polychord* is a structure which has two complete chords.

It is built from the chosen chord scale; the two structures create a high degree of tension; the spacing between the two chords is critical:

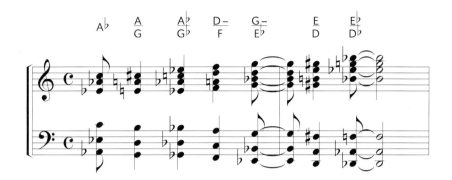

The two measures above (the end of the B section of "The Duke") are harmonizations using polychords. Notice how there is an increase of complexity from the beginning of the phrase to the end. Also, notice the contrapuntal relationship of the melody to the root motion. These are often common factors where polychords are found. Indeed, it is not unusual to find polychords which are not derived using a specific chord scale, but are designed solely to produce an increase in tension. The control of the tension is governed by the intervals between the individual notes of the upper structure to the lower structure. Minor 7 and major 9 intervals are *consonant*; major 7 and minor 9 intervals are *dissonant*:

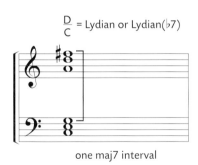

one maj7 interval

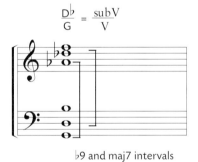

♭9 and maj7 intervals

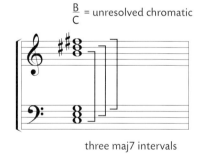

three maj7 intervals

PEDAL POINT - OSTINATO

W̲here pedal point is found, there will appear to be inversions and/or hybrids. However, pedal point is not a vertical, but a linear consideration:

or:

A *pedal point* (also called organ point) utilizes the tonic and/or dominant pitches of the key as *tonic* pedal and/or *dominant* pedal, as a *bass* pedal (below the harmonies as demonstrated above), an *internal* pedal (inside the harmonies), or a *soprano* pedal (above the harmonies). It may be rhythmic, or sustained:

Internal dominant pedal:

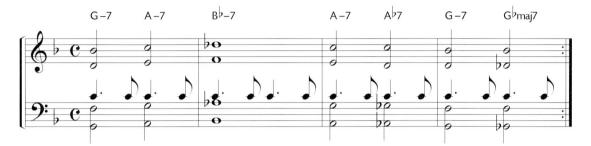

Soprano tonic and dominant pedal:

Ostinato is an elaborate form of pedal point. An ostinato is a repeated melodic figure which begins with a pedal. The pitches of the melodic figure may change to accommodate the chords, or in a more pure ostinato, repeat exactly. An ostinato finds a favorite use in the A sections of "On Green Dolphin Street."

Fixed ostinato:

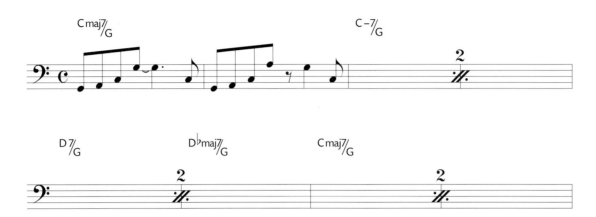

Changing ostinato:

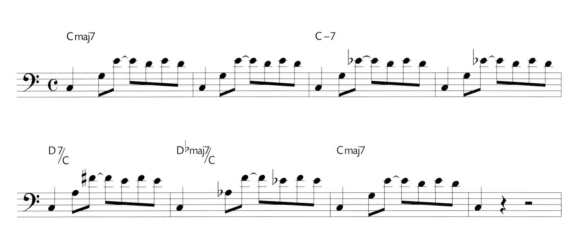

Layered ostinato uses an ostinato figure and has added increasing rhythmic interest:

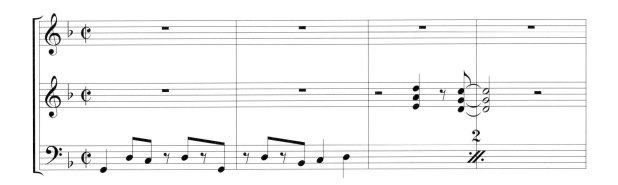

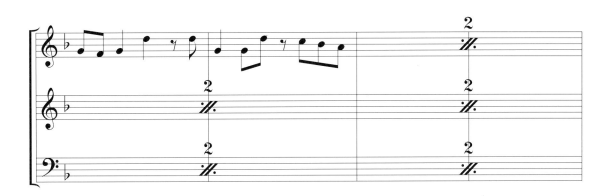

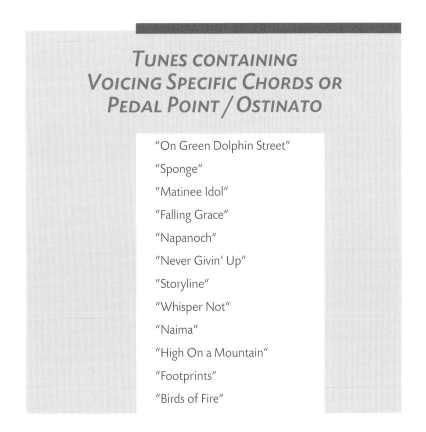

TUNES CONTAINING VOICING SPECIFIC CHORDS OR PEDAL POINT / OSTINATO

"On Green Dolphin Street"

"Sponge"

"Matinee Idol"

"Falling Grace"

"Napanoch"

"Never Givin' Up"

"Storyline"

"Whisper Not"

"Naima"

"High On a Mountain"

"Footprints"

"Birds of Fire"

10
Modulations

or this chapter it is recommended that lead sheets of the following tunes be gathered for reference when mentioned in the text.

"The Dolphin"	"Pensativa"
"Dolphin Dance"	"Softly"
"The Girl From Ipanema"	"The Song Is You"
"Here's That Rainy Day"	"You Go To My Head"
"I'm All Smiles"	"Waltz for Debby"
"Lady Sings the Blues"	"Watch What Happens"
"Like Someone In Love"	"What's New?"
"Lover"	"Why Did I Choose You?"

CONSIDERATIONS

A *modulation* occurs when the tonal or modal center is transposed to a new tonal or modal center. The listener's focus *must* change from the original tonic reference to the new secondary reference. Many tunes do not modulate ("My Romance," "A Foggy Day," "I Got Rhythm").

Modulations can be categorized as being *implied* or *actual*; *subtle*, if to a closely related key or *acute*, if to a distant key. The keys closest to the originating key are the keys of IV and V because there is only one accidental difference ("Why Did I Choose You?," "What's New?"). The keys most distant from the original are a half step higher (key of ♭II) and a half step lower (key of VII) because they contain 7 accidental differences ("The Girl From Ipanema"). For purposes of this chapter, the secondary keys will be referenced to the originating key. Therefore, "The Girl From Ipanema" moves between the keys of I (F), ♭VI (D♭), VII (E) and back to I (F).

Modal interchange between parallel keys is not perceived as modulation because the tonal reference remains. However, there are common modulations which have a modal relationship with the original key. The key of ♭III is very often heard as a secondary key because it represents the relative major of the original tonic's natural minor and contains common diatonic chords ("Softly," "Here's That Rainy Day"). The same relation exists between the original tonic key and the key of VI (relative/parallel keys) ("Pensativa," "Like Someone In Love").

Chapter 10

When analyzing a modulation, parentheses (indicating a change of function or deceptive resolution resulting in a modulation) may be present. In some highly sophisticated circumstances, a modulation may occur for only one chord. (The first chord of the bridge of "Pensativa" is ♭IImaj7 in B major and Imaj7 in C. The previous chord is V7/IV in G♭ and V7/I in B. The key of B is never consummated, only implied.)

In lead sheet notation, it is common practice to use accidentals instead of formally changing the key signature ("Body and Soul" is an exception). The accidentals and the enharmonic spelling for the chord symbols is governed by reading ease as opposed to the actual directional sound of the modulation. (For example, if the original key were C and the modulation were up a half step, it will not be written in C♯, because D♭ is easier to visualize.) Some lead sheets may be seen that use the key signature of the last key and not the original key. ("Quiet Nights" is notated in C major, which is the final key, but the originating key is F.) Indeed, some lead sheets use a key signature that accommodates the bulk of the melody pitches but does not represent the key of the harmonies. This is especially true of blues. ("Good-bye Pork Pie Hat" is a blues in F but the key signature is F minor. "Minority" is a 16 bar minor harmony blues but the melody is written in major.)

Tunes that modulate will often demonstrate a harmonic pattern of keys as in "My Little Boat" (keys of I, ♭VII, ♭VI, back to I).

Within tunes we have been conditioned to expect a return to the original key after a modulation, which usually occurs.

Upward modulations are favored by arrangers because they force forward movement of the music and are most often used to generate excitement and variety. (Listen to almost any Barry Manilow or Stevie Wonder arrangement.)

It is *not* necessary for a new tonic chord to be heard after a modulation. Establishment of the new key can be accomplished by the melody and/or the harmonies without overtly stating tonic function.

If the melody modulates into a new key, the harmonies must modulate (again, the bridge of "The Girl From Ipanema"). However, it is not necessary for the melody to instigate the modulation if the harmonies define a new key. The melody will modulate by default ("I'm All Smiles").

DIRECT

irect modulations most often occur after the I chord because if represents a point of harmonic finality. Either the original I chord or the new key's tonic will have a change of function, but the governing factor is the relationship between the keys ("I'm All Smiles"):

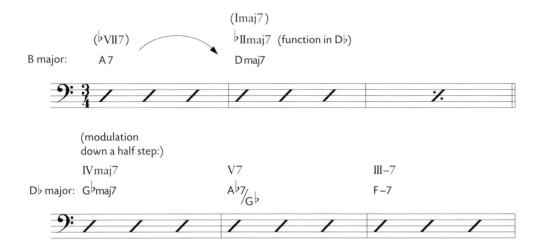

Less frequently, a direct modulation will occur from the diatonic II, III, IV, V, or VI chords. These direct modulations will be by step or half step and there will not be a functional harmonic relationship in the original key ("Waltz for Debby"):

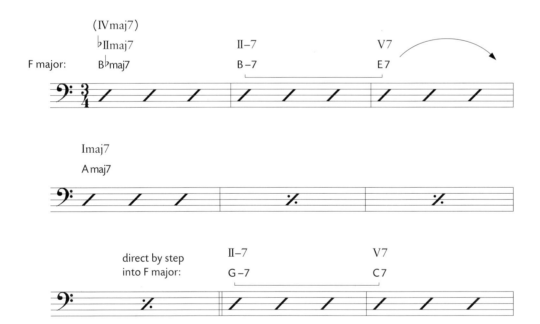

Any modulation from the diatonic V7 chord will probably be associated with deceptive resolution. However, the melody may affect a modulation, forcing the V7 chord to modulate directly without resolving. This is an often used arranging device:

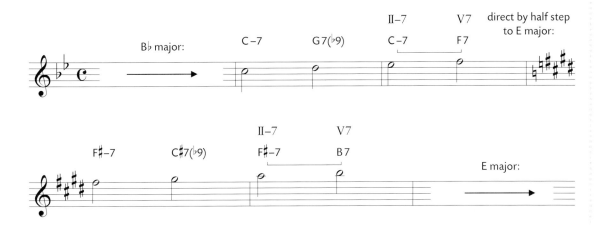

Another very typical arranging modulation involves the V7 of the original key moving nonfunctionally to the V7 of the new key. The *chord scales* used dictate the new key to the listener:

In the above, either the melody drives the modulation, or the relationship between the two keys controls. The same nonfunctional relationships occur when a modulation is chromatically direct ("Watch What Happens"):

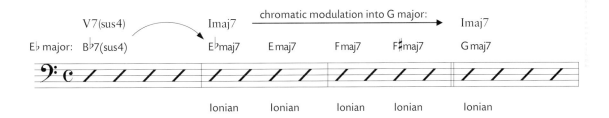

Though each chord may be seen as a ♭IImaj7 in the key of the previous chord, to the listener the ascending chords are forcing a modulation into the new key, therefore, nonfunctional analysis. The chord scales used for the chromatic chords will be the same as the scales for the neighboring chords of tonic E♭maj7 and Gmaj7.

<table>
<tr><td>PIVOT CHORD</td><td>Chords which change function between the originating key and the secondary key are *pivot chords*. The chord's new function becomes apparent in retrospect as the new key unfolds ("Dolphin Dance"):</td></tr>
</table>

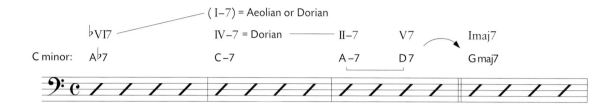

The change of function is indicated through the use of parenthetical analysis which shows the original function and hence, the chord scale. The analysis not in parentheses (this includes the arrow indicating perfect 5th or half step resolution) is the function in the new key. As an example, C–7 may have a pivot function as I–7 (as above), II–7, III–7, IV–7 (as above), V–7, or VI–7. (The rare functions referred to in the chapter about modal interchange are usually not seen where pivot chords are found.) The choice of chord scale is most often dictated by the pivot chord's initial or original key function, creating an unexpected modulation. However, the chord scale for the new key is also available.

<table>
<tr><td>DOMINANT</td><td>Deceptive resolutions of dominant chords are very common methods used to achieve modulations. The multiplicity of dominant functions allows for modulation into any key. Any dominant chord has the capability of moving deceptively using any *intervalic root motion*:</td></tr>
</table>

Down a:

perfect 5	to a new Imaj7 ("I'm All Smiles");
tritone	as V7/I to ♭IImaj7 ("Pensativa");
perfect 4th	as IV7 to Imaj7 ("Lady Sings the Blues");
major 3rd	as V7/I to ♭IIImaj7 ("Softly");
minor 3rd (unusual)	as V7/I to the root of III–7 becoming a new Imaj7 ("Pure Imagination");
step (unusual)	as II7 to Imaj7 ("Imagination");
half step	as subV7 to Imaj7 ("The Dolphin")

Up a:

half step	as VII7 to Imaj7 ("The Song Is You");
step	as ♭VII7 to Imaj7 ("Pensativa");
minor 3rd (unusual)	as VI7 to Imaj7 ("Killer Joe");
major 3rd	as ♭VI7 to Imaj7 ("Lady Sings the Blues")

Secondary dominant chords are very common in deceptive resolution modulations. A new tonic is found in place of the expected diatonic chord (*change of expected chord quality*) following V7/II, V7/III, V7/V, V7/VI. (Because the IVmaj7 chord contains the *same chord quality* as a tonic Imaj7, this type modulation does not apply.) ("I'm All Smiles"):

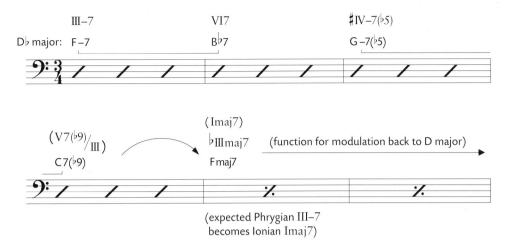

(The Fmaj7 above represents another single chord modulation.)

A *transitional modulation* is achieved by losing the original tonality through the use of nondiatonic functioning dominant chords in a cycle. The related II–7 chords may also be present. Transitional modulations are another common arranging device:

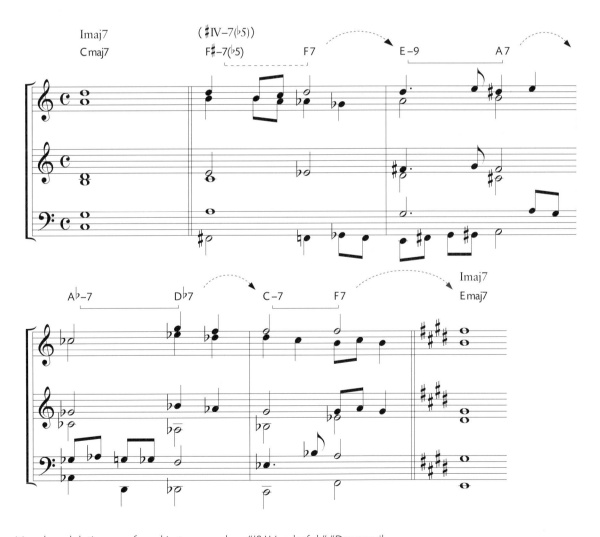

Transitional modulations are found in tunes such as "'S Wonderful," "Dreamsville," "You Never Give Me Your Money." The melodic character in transitional modulations is usually static or sequential.

11
Modal Systems

CHARACTER
NOTES

All the diatonic modes have one thing in common, they contain the same seven pitches arranged in different order. Dorian, Phrygian, Aeolian, Lydian, and Mixolydian are *displacements* of the major mode – the Ionian scale. Each mode's characteristic is distinct from the others by the specific location within the mode of one particular pitch – the *character note*. In the *Ionian* mode/scale, the ♮4th scale degree is the character note:

tritone

The *Lydian* mode character note is the ♯4 scale degree which distinguishes it from Ionian:

tritone

The *Mixolydian* mode differs from the other major modes in that the character note is the ♭7 scale degree:

tritone

The character note of *Aeolian* is the ♭6th scale degree:

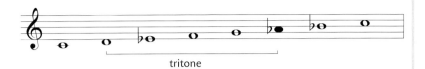

Dorian differs from Aeolian because the character note is a ♮6 scale degree:

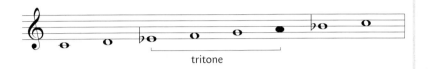

Phrygian differs from the above minor modes with a ♭2 scale degree character note:

Any diatonic chords which contain the character note as a chord tone are *very unstable*, and therefore will progress to the more stable chords which do not contain the character note as a chord tone. Because of the position of the character note, Locrian has always been ignored as a modal system. The *Locrian* mode has the paradox of finding the *unstable* characteristic pitch, scale degree ♭5, as a chord tone of the *stable* tonic chord:

An observation of the modes reveals that the character notes are one of the two pitches making up the diatonic tritone. In a major or minor key, the tritone has the important function of creating the primary cadential sound. In a modal context, the tritone must be carefully controlled in order to retain the modal character while not lapsing into the relative major or minor key. The character note of the mode locates half of the diatonic tritone, and must be present. For this reason, there are certain avoided diatonic chord structures which inherently contain both pitches of the tritone. *The diatonic –7(♭5) is avoided*. The diatonic *dominant 7th chord* is most often treated as a *triad*, avoiding the use of both tritone notes. Each of the five common modes contain seven different pitches and six diatonic chords.

Chord Progressions

Lead sheets of modal tunes do not always contain a modal progression – simply the name of the mode. An understanding of modal harmonies may prove helpful for writers and rhythm section players.

The diatonic chords of the mode can be divided into three functional areas:

- The *tonic* chord of the mode stands alone.

- The *cadential* chords are those diatonic 7th chords and the diatonic triad which contain, as a chord tone, the characteristic pitch.

- The *noncadential* chords do not contain the character note as a chord tone.

(For the following examples, T = tonic, C = cadence chord, the noncadential chords are not labelled.)

The functions for the diatonic chords of Lydian are:

The functions for the diatonic chords of Mixolydian are:

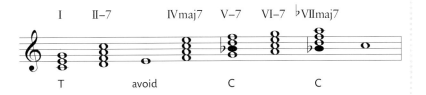

The functions for the diatonic chords of Dorian are:

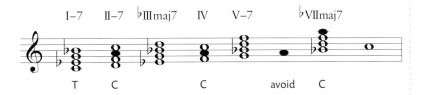

The functions for the diatonic chords of Phrygian are:

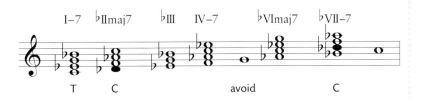

The functions for the diatonic chords of Aeolian are:

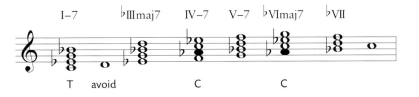

The organization of a modal progression takes into account the following considerations:

- The strongest cadential motion of major key, minor key, and blues is root motion of perfect fifths or its inversion, perfect fourths, typical of dominant or subdominant root motion. The typical root motion found in modal harmony is synonymous with mode/scale–*steps*.

- A cadence by step is *not* possible in Aeolian.

- The position of the character pitch within the cadence chords will determine the comparative strength for each chord. The characteristic pitch as the root has the *greatest* demand for resolution; as the 5th is *next strongest*; as the 3rd is *weak*; and as the 7th is *weakest*.

- The tonic chord receives the most *stress*.

- Cadences are from *weak* beats.

- *Simplicity is important when dealing with modal systems.*

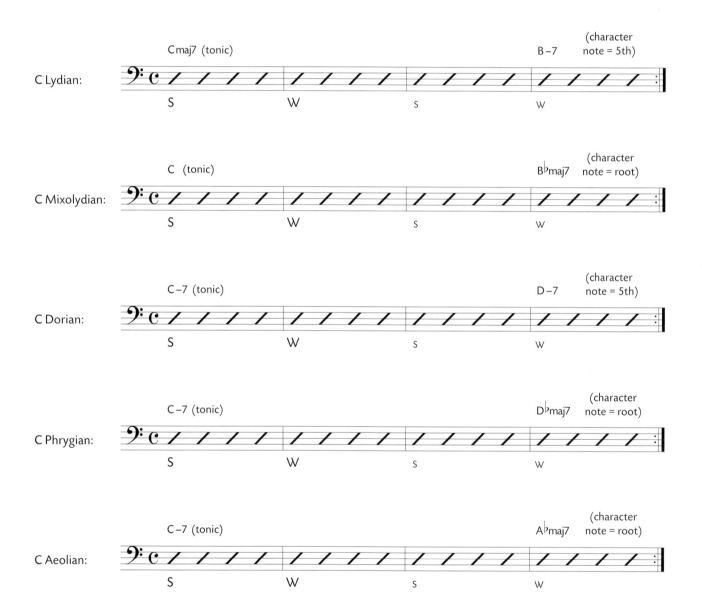

If a more complex progression is desired (but usually not necessary), or if the melody demands a different chord, the cadence chord can be preceded by a *noncadential* chord; that chord can then be preceded by a cadence chord and so on. The cadence chords will continue falling on weak stress points ultimately cadencing to tonic:

The available tensions for the diatonic modal chords are a whole step above a chord tone. For the diatonic Dorian chord scale, 13 *is* an available tension. The diatonic tritone need not be avoided if one pitch is a tension; this is not perceived as a dominant sound. Because all the notes of Dorian and Lydian are available on the I chord, the total sound of the mode is self-contained and a cadence to tonic is unnecessary:

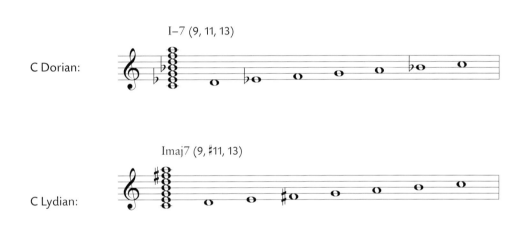

In addition to the diatonic chords built in thirds, *hybrids* are available. Each individual hybrid will function as either a cadence or noncadence chord based on the inclusion or omission of the character note. Maj6 is an alternative for the diatonic maj7 chords.

MELODIES

M odal melodies contain the following attributes:

- They are almost always *diatonic*.

- Chromatics may appear as *simple* passing tone ornamentations.

- Like typical modal root motion, *steps* are common.

- *Arpeggios* of the diatonic chords and consecutive leaps of *4ths* are typical.

- Cadences are most often by step and resolve to either scale degrees 1 or 5 (or 3).

- The character note is often found *emphasized*.

- *Many* or *all* the pitches of the mode will be heard.

- The diatonic *tritone* is neither outlined (top and bottom notes of a melodic motif) nor leaped (except in a series of consecutive 4ths). In either case, the tritone is *never* resolved by traditional means.

- The key signature may be *open* (no key signature), or the key for the *relative* major/minor, or (least desirable) the key for the *parallel* major/minor. The actual modality is *indicated*.

MODAL TUNES TO ANALYZE
WHICH DEMONSTRATE THE ABOVE

"It's a Lazy Afternoon"

"Black Narcissus"

"Crystal Silence"

"Follow Your Heart"

"Little Sunflower"

"Maiden Voyage"

"Moondance"

"Norwegian Wood"

"Recordame"

"Simone"

"So What"

"Milestones"

"Little B's Poem"

"First Light"

"Darkness"

"Tell Me a Bedtime Story"

"Saga of Harrison Crabfeathers"

"Footprints"

Chord structures used for modal harmonies and in support of modal melodies are:

- often triadic, or triads with added color tone (tension);

C Dorian:

- or quartal (voiced in fourths);

C Dorian:

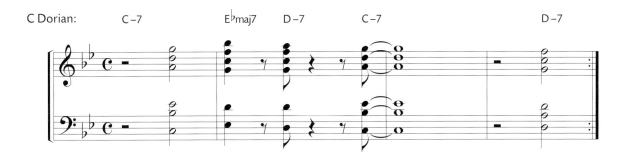

- may be diatonically parallel (as some of the above);
- may be pandiatonic/tonic modal voicings.

Pandiatonicism is the use of diatonic structures to achieve the harmonic sound of the key/mode without emphasizing a single pitch as the tonic. Tonic modal voicings, most often in fourths, are a convenient way for a writer, or chordal instrument player, to create an illusion of a modal progression where only the tonic modal chord is indicated. Tonic modal voicings will each sound tonic and carry equal weigh when moving in parallel motion:

C Dorian:

Pedal point and ostinato (see above) are very typically found in modal music because of the strength of scale degrees 1 and 5 (tonic and dominant pedals).

Polymodality is the simultaneous use of two or more different modes, or two or more different modal centers.

For example, a C Dorian melody supported with a C Phrygian harmony part:

Or a C Dorian melody supported with an A Dorian harmony part (parallelism):

Counterpoint may be developed using polymodality or the melody and harmonies may appear in different keys/modes (the introduction to "Tell Me a Bedtime Story").

The foregoing information is an overview of basic modal concepts. Those interested may continue further explorations into the topic by analyzing the music of the Brecker Brothers, Wayne Shorter, Chick Corea, John McLaughlin, Michael Gibbs, and other composers of the same genre, as well as experimentation with the modes of harmonic or melodic minor and other synthetic scales.

12
Non-functional Harmony

The chapter about modulations introduced situations which were *nonfunctional*. The controlling force was not the key, as is the case for functional progressions, but the melody or the relationship between chords.

Nonfunctional harmony has its basis in *symmetry*. Diatonic major key, minor key, blues, and the modal systems have, as a commonality, diatonic scales and chord scales which are not symmetric (with the exception of the whole-tone, symmetric dominant, and symmetric diminished chord scales). Where symmetry exists, nonfunctional relationships usually exist. The simple symmetric relationships which divide the octave are:

2 tritone intervals:

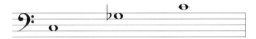

3 major 3rd intervals:

4 minor 3rd intervals:

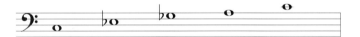

6 major 2nd intervals:

12 minor 2nd intervals:

When chords progress or keys move by a continual symmetry, a graphic and/or semantic analysis must be used to rationalize the event. *Multitonic* tunes can be analyzed functionally, however, the glue which holds them together is the symmetry of relationship. For example, John Coltrane's "Giant Steps" is a nonfunctional tune based on symmetric keys a major 3rd apart:

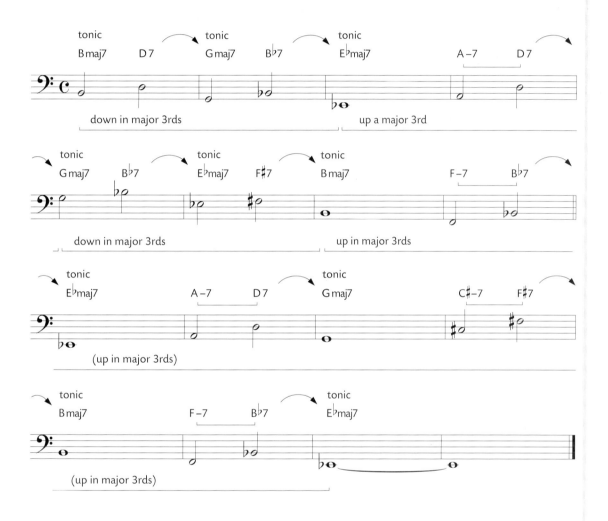

- There are three tonal centers, spaced a major 3rd (minor 6th) apart (B, G, E♭).
- The melody is symmetric.
- All three tonics carry equal weight.
- Each dominant 7th chord is a primary dominant.
- The tune could end on any tonic and sound final.
- A functional analysis is possible, but misses the point; graphics and words are used.

Here "Giant Steps" is analyzed functionally:

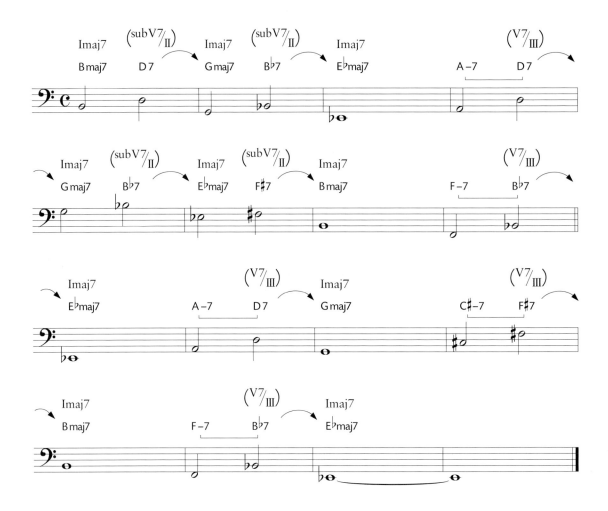

The choices for the chord scales of a multitonic tune such as "Giant Steps" would normally reflect the diatonic of each individual tonal center (Ionian, Mixolydian, and Dorian respectively for the Imaj7, V7, and II–7 chords above). As a player, these are the scales used by John Coltrane for his impovisation. However, because each tonic is as strong as the others, and the relationship between the three tonalities is symmetric, a choice of Lydian, Lydian ♭7, and Dorian for the same chords is potential (especially for comping players and arrangers).

Many tunes rely on this symmetric relationship but in a functional way. "Pensativa" is an example of a composition in which the modulatory development is based on an incomplete 4-tonic system utilizing functional harmonic progressions. "I'll Remember April" is a standard tune with a bridge also based on an incomplete 4-tonic system. Many standards contain a tonally unstable bridge where symmetrical relations may appear, as in "Have You Met Miss Jones" (3-tonic system):

The functional application of symmetrical relationships traces back to the 19th century when dominant harmony (tonic dominant relation) had reached its limitation and chromatic mediant harmony (relationships in thirds) and other symmetrical devices (whole-tone, chromatic) had gained more interest. These should not be confused with simple root progression in thirds and seconds, which were common for a long time past. Symmetry and chromatic third relations produce an extension of tonality which lead to loosening the tonal center. Composers like Schubert and Wagner used multitonic systems, mostly functional, as harmonic goals of modulations.

It is known that John Coltrane studied the music of the 19th century and adapted it for his purposes. He composed and reharmonized tunes based on standards applying multitonic systems: "Tune Up" by Miles Davis became the reharmonization "Countdown" and "How High The Moon" became "Satellite." He also reharmonized Gershwin's "But Not For Me."

CONTIGUOUS DOMINANTS

Nonfunctional progressions are also found in predominantly functional tunes. The most common occurrence are *contiguous dominants* – dominants with or without their related II–7 chords which appear next to each other but not functioning to each other. The most common contiguous dominant chords have a common expectation to resolve to chords of *similar* function (such as the dominants of tonic chords – V7/I, V7/III, V7/VI) as in "Alone Together":

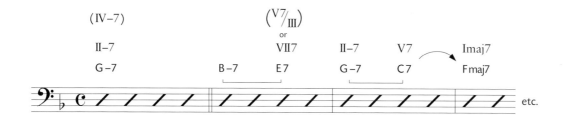

Also in this group will be found dominant chords which have an expectation for a common *resolution* chord (V7 and ♭VII7) as in "The Dolphin":

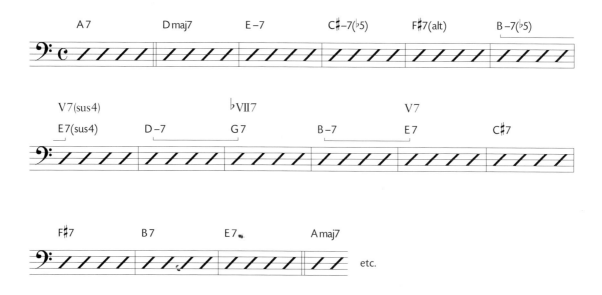

Importantly, the above contiguous dominants do not progress as dominant to dominant, but to a *common expectation*. Contiguous dominants come from common practice in functional harmony but are used in nonfunctional settings. Therefore, it is possible for a functional analysis to be used, but it will not describe the actual sound of the progression and the most appropriate chord scales (see "I'm All Smiles" below).

Dominant resolution is usually heard downward. However, contiguous dominants describe a root motion *upward* by half step, step, minor 3rd, or major 3rd.

Root motion *upward by half step* for contiguous dominants may have originated as an arranging technique for extending the final cadence to tonic by V7 moving to its subV7/V and back to V7:

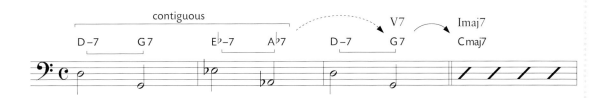

Typical of contiguous dominant progressions, any dominant chord may have any resolution. The above subV7/V can move with any root motion to any chord. Therefore the subV7/V may resolve as a V7/I ("Moment's Notice"):

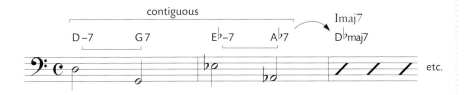

Root motion by *whole step upward* is typical of the deceptive resolution of V7/I to III–7. When heard in a continually ascending setting, the resulting chords are contiguous dominants and will have an expectation to continue to ascend until a final resolution takes place ("I'm All Smiles"):

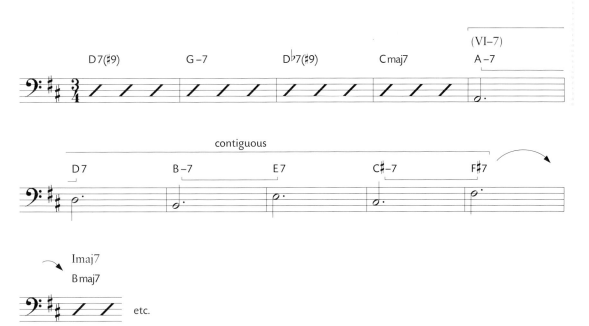

Contiguous dominant root motion *upward in minor 3rds* is functionally found as V7 to ♭VII7 (dominant/subdominant minor cadence) as in "The Dolphin" above. The contiguous dominant chords may be implied. The result will be *contiguous II–7 chords* as in the last section of "The Shadow Of Your Smile":

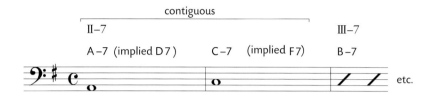

Contiguous dominant root motion *upward by major 3rd* intervals can be traced to the V7 of tonic I moving to V7 of tonic III–7 (see "Alone Together" above). This is also typical of V7 indirectly resolving after the reharmonization for the I°7 chord (V7/I to VII7 as sometimes used for the beginning of "Misty"):

The chord scales for contiguous dominants and their related II–7 chords will be, especially for the player, Dorian/Mixolydian. However, some freedom exists (especially when the related II–7 is not present), because one is dealing with dominant chords whose expectation is not to resolve down a perfect fifth, therefore Lydian♭7. Where the contiguous dominant progresses in a continual pattern, an option is to use the chord scale for the first chord of the series. *Symmetric dominant* is a particularly good chord scale choice for *symmetric* nonfunctional *dominant* chords.

A contiguous dominant progression can contain added interpolated functional motion. This complexity will have both written and graphic analysis. .

Chords of the *same quality* which move in a *constant* root pattern are *constant structures*. The consistency of root motion is commonly 3rds but other intervals may be seen. The chords may be any quality, although −7(♭5) chords are rare:

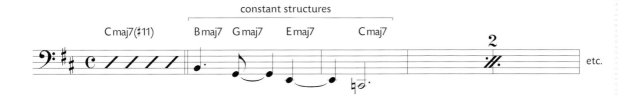

Herbie Hancock's "Tell Me a Bedtime Story" above contains an interesting constant structure progression. The root motion is constantly 3rds (major or minor) and the chords are all maj7. Notice that the roots spell, in retrograde, the chord tones of the prior Cmaj7 chord. The chord progression does not sound functional, but it is possible to functionally justify the chords in B major as Imaj7, ♭VImaj7, IVmaj7, ♭IImaj7. The chord scales should than be constant Ionian. However, as with other nonfunctional situations a functional analysis will not define the most correct chord scale choices. The chord scales best used are *Lydian* because there is no specific tonic chord in control of the pattern.

Constant structures may be based on root motion (as above) or constantly *linked to the melody* (parallel) – listen to the chromatic approach chord possibilities in the first 4 measures of "White Christmas." In this reharmonization of "Here's That Rainy Day," the 2nd and 6th measures are constant structures driven by the melody:

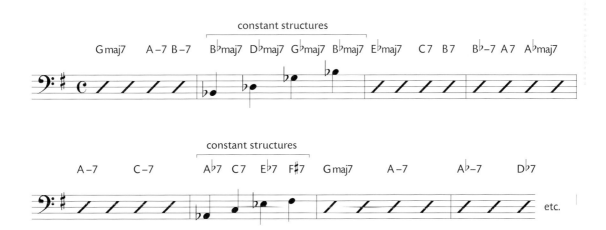

Recall, when diminished chords are found nonfunctionally, the chord scale will be symmetric diminished as in "Little Niles":

PATTERNED CHORD
PROGRESSIONS

Much the same as the end result of the study of species counterpoint is free counterpoint, the end result of the analysis of harmonic progressions is the concept of any chord moving to any other chord. The requirement is the utilization of *control*. In progressions which contain a nonfunctional pattern of harmonic activity, the control is applied to the pattern by repetition or development.

An example of a *repeated patterned chord progression* is "Tones For Joan's Bones." A pattern of chords is established and then repeated. Typical of repeated patterned material, the pattern occurs three times, after which it is changed in order to allow for the resolution of tension built by repetition:

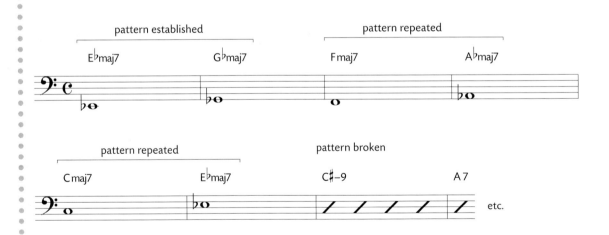

Patterns can be linked by any interval. In the above example, the linking intervals are 1/2 step and major 3rd.

The pattern may be quite short and *developed*. "Time Remembered" is based on the opening statement of −7 moving up a half step to maj7. The initial development is in transposed retrograde:

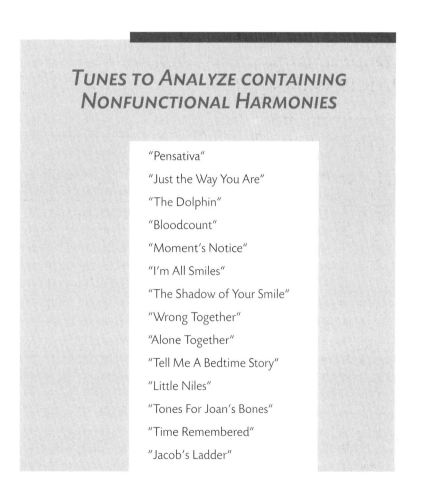

13

Introduction
to
Arranging

A surface overview of arranging and orchestration principles used in the harmonization process will help to understand how harmonies are organized. There are three primary methods for voicing chords. Each is dependent on one of the following:

- melodic function
- root motion
- instrumental limitations

Harmonizations based on the melody are typical in jazz and jazz influenced styles. The melody is the most important function. The supporting harmonies are secondary:

This melodically driven technique is called **block style** or **4-way close**. The melody represents a pitch from the chord scale. The other pitches are the remaining notes of the chord. The melody will be:

- a chord tone,
- a tension
- an avoid note,
- or an embellishment resolving to an available chord tone or tension.

Each of these situations is treated differently:

- If a melody note is a chord tone, add the remaining notes of the chord to produce a complete chord sound. (See the above example.)

- If a melody note is a tension, the chord tone directly beneath the tension is omitted and the remaining notes of the chord are added producing a complete chord sound:

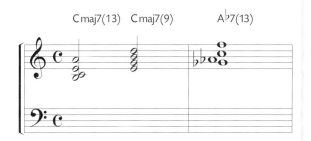

- If a melodic note is a harmonic avoid note, the supporting notes may be sustained chord sound (referred to as **independent lead**). This allows the avoid note to resolve itself. The other solution is to use pitches that resolve, along with the melody, to a predetermined target voicing based on the available pitches of the chord scale. (This is referred to as **approach note reharmonization**):

independent lead

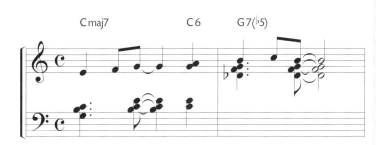

approach note reharmonization

• The previous methods also apply when the melody is any form of chromatic embellishment of the chord scale. It is also possible to view any diatonic note from the chord scale as a melodic approach note so long as it resolves to an available chord tone or tension:

Additional mechanical harmonization techniques based on 4-way close are:

- drop 2:   Four-way close with the second voice from the top positioned an octave lower),

- drop 3:   Four-way close with the third voice from the top positioned an octave lower, and

- drop 2 and 4:   Four-way close with the second and fourth voices from the top positioned an octave lower.

Typical of all these techniques is the substitution of tension 9 (if available) for the root (the bass player is paid to play the root), or tension 13 or ♭13 (if available) for the 5th (which is most often considered the least important note of the 7th chord):

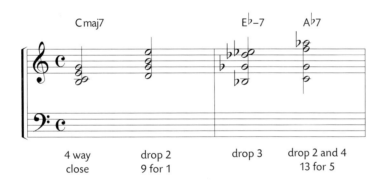

The limitations of instrumentation and range effect the use of any of the above voicings. These harmonizations are so dependent on the melody that it is common for the melody to be doubled (usually below the harmonies). George Shearing made this a popular jazz style and even quadrupled the melody with vibes and guitar.

This harmonization method inherently produces similar and parallel movement; *parallel 5ths and octaves are permitted, expected, and are therefore required.*

Root position voicings or spreads are common to contemporary harmonies. Unlike voicings dictated by the melody, these structures tend to follow more traditional lines. The following example will demonstrate a relatively tame harmonization of a short chord progression with no implied melody:

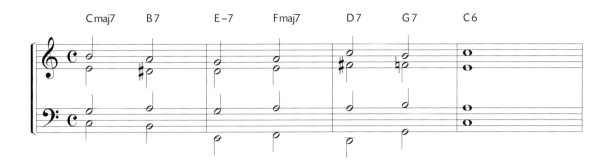

The next example is more complicated:

Both examples are root position, therefore, some generalities can be stated:

- Roots and 5ths appear in the *lower* voices or higher.

- *Chord sound* (the 3rds and 7ths) occupy *middle* ground or higher.

- Tensions are in the *upper* voices.

- The larger adjacent intervals are reserved for the lower areas; smaller adjacent intervals are higher.

- Melodic motion in any voice requires a more traditional approach to contrapuntal relationships.

- All approach notes and avoid notes resolve; tensions resolve or become suspended into a chord tone or another tension.

The considerations above can be seen as having their basis in the *overtone series* and the basic human need for resolution of tension. Additional observations will shed some light on how spreads are realized:

- The tritones of the dominant chords do not necessarily resolve in the traditional manner.

- Parallel motion is typical, not avoided.

- The 5th of the chords can be omitted.

- The doubling of any pitch is common.

- The texture can be controlled from "thin" to "thick" sounding voicings.

This is traditional voice leading advanced by 200 years. Contemporary jazz harmonies have reached such a level of complexity that it is possible to find examples of harmonic structures containing all 12 notes of the chromatic scale.

Root position structures often support higher close position harmonies because that combination will follow the intervals found in the overtone series. (Henry Mancini was fond of this kind of harmonization for his "brass choir" of 4 French horns and 4 trombones. Listen to his composition "Dreamsville".)

Instrumentation effects the way chords are voiced. A guitar player would be stressed to play any of the previous examples due to the nature of the instrument; one hand to manipulate six strings tuned mostly in 4ths. On the other hand, a pianist has ten possible note choices, but there is a limit to the span from the little finger to the thumb. The last example is playable by a professional choir of six trombones, or six saxophones, but six trumpets could not do it.

Refer to *Modal Systems, Voicing Specific Chord Symbols and Structures* and *Nonfunctional Harmony* chapters for additional harmonization techniques.

A study of basic instrumentation and orchestration is beyond the scope of this book. However, it is obvious that for different instrumentations, different harmonizations are necessary. The examples found in this book are all generic; no specific instrumentation is intended or implied.

T his appendix is a concise guide to the understanding and application of technical terms used in this book and in the professional musical world. More detailed information can be found in the corresponding chapters.

Approach Note Reharmonization: Harmonization technique; a chord using pitches that resolve to a predetermined target voicing based on the appropriate chord scale.

Avoid Notes: The pitch or pitches of a chord scale which are not used harmonically because they will destabilize the sound of the chord.

Example: The avoid note of a major tonic chord is the perfect 4th, which can not coexist with the major third (in tonal harmony), because suspension and resolution would sound at the same time. The melody may use this pitch as a non-chord tone (passing tone, neighboring tone, ...).

Ballad: Slow tune.

Beat: The basic pulse.

Blue Notes: Originally only the minor third and the minor seventh in a major tonality: the blues tonality. Contemporary blues also includes the ♭5 = ♯4 (♯11).

Bones = Trombones

Borrowed Chords: Chords taken from a different tonality or modality.

Break: An interruption in the accompaniment, usually maintaining the underlying beat and harmonic progression.

Bridge: The B section of a tune.

Changes: See *Chord Changes*.

Chart: Written arrangement; sheet music.

Chord Scale Theory: The relationship of scales to certain chords and vice versa. Scales are derived from extended chord structures (13th chords) by dropping notes down one octave (if they exceed one octave) and by reordering them in seconds. The appropriate scale for a given chord is determined by the function of the chord.

Chord Scales: Chord scales have three basic qualities:
1. Chord Tones: The most stable pitches. In jazz the basic chord structure is the seventh chord built in thirds (root=1, third=3, fifth=5, seventh=7)
2. Tensions: Additional tones by extending the chord in thirds.
3. Avoid Notes: Pitches, which sound very dissonant and therefore are avoided harmonically.

Chorus: The main body of a tune. Typical common forms are AB, ABA, AABA, ABAC.

Cluster: Three or more pitches in secundal relationship played simultaneously (Secundal Harmony). The term "cluster" was coined by the American composer Henry Cowell.

Common Chord: See *Pivot Chord*.

Comping: Chordal accompaniment for a soloist, mostly interactive and improvised.

Conditional Avoid Notes: They occur in Mixolydian ♭13 chord scales. The 5th and the ♭13th are conditional to the use of each other to maintain the clear character of a chord. They are available melodically (see *Secondary Dominants*).

Constant Structures: Chords of the same quality moving in a consistent root motion pattern.

Contiguous Dominants: Dominant chords (with or without their related II–7 chords) which appear next to each other but not functioning to each other.

Double Time: The real doubling of the tempo and the metric pulse. Chord changes are twice as fast.

Double-Time Feel: The apparent doubling of the tempo, the original harmonic rhythm stays the same.

Dorian Avoid Note: An exception to avoid note criteria. 13 is avoided harmonically on the II–7 in order to reserve the dominant tritone for the related V7.

Drop 2, Drop 3, Drop 2 and 4: Four-way close with the respective pitch(es) placed an octave lower creating open position harmonies.

Extended Dominants: See *Sequential Dominants*

Fill In, Fill: An additional rhythmic or melodic phrase played during a break or a transition.

Fours: See *Trade*.

Four-Way Close: A harmonization technique used for active, fast melodies. The melody is harmonized by three other voices creating a voicing in close position.

Functional Harmony: An analytical theory method which categorizes all chords into basic sound groups.

Groove: The interaction of rhythm and time.

Guide Tones, Guide Tone Lines: The essence of a chord progression distilled from the voice leading of each chord's basic sound. There are two lines generated; one is often the basic voice leading of the melody.

Harmonic Rhythm: The rate of chord change.

Head: The theme of a tune (melody and chords).

Head Arrangement: An ad hoc arrangement created spontaneously during performance.

Hybrids: See *Slash Chords*.

Independent Lead: Harmonization technique: If the melodic note is a harmonic avoid note or a chromatic embellishment of the chord scale, the supporting notes may be sustained chord sound allowing the melodic note to resolve itself.

Interchange Chords: Chords which can in addition or to replace others of similar function.

Intro = Introduction.

Lead Sheet: A score, in manuscript or printed form, showing only a composition's melody, its corresponding chords (written above the melody), and sometimes the lyrics.

Line Cliché: A single chromatic line during an otherwise static chord. The notes invloved occurin the area where the chord's seventh would normally be and create the illusion of harmonic motion.

Low Interval Limits: An acoustic phenomenon imposed by the inability to hear a chord function other than root or fifth in the extreme low register for chords built in root position.

Modal Interchange: Borrowing chords from parallel tonalities/modalities for use in the primary key.

Multitonic Systems: Harmonies and melodies resulting in more than one tonal center. Symmentrical tonal relationship will exist.

N.C. = No Chord.

Nonfunctional Harmony: Progressions, or portions of progressions, where the controlling factor is not the key or the tonality, but the chords relationship to one another or the melody.

Octatonic Scale: An 8-tone scale.

Offbeats: Notes, accents played between the beats.

Outro: (Not universal.) The end of an arrangement using the material from the introduction.

Pandiatonicism: The use of diatonic structures to achieve the harmonic sound of the key/mode without emphasizing a single pitch as the tonic.

Pentatonic Scale: A five-tone scale without half steps.

Pivot Chord (also: Common Chord): A chord which has functions in more than one key.

Polychords: One chord above another. Complex chord structures can thus be simply notated.

E.g., $\dfrac{\text{D}\flat}{\text{G7}}$ D♭ triad over G7

Polymodality: See *Modal Harmony.*

Primary Dominant: The dominant chord which precedes the tonic: V7/I.

Quartal, Quintal Harmony: Chords built in fourths (mostly perfect, sometimes augmented) or fifths. They can function as substitutes for tertian chords, but have a characteristical, strong and ambiguous sound. No specific, common symbols exist.

Related II–7: Not only the primary dominant V7 may be preceded by its diatonic subdominant II–7, but any dominant may be preceded by its related II–7.

Retrograde: Backwards.

Rhythm Changes: A non-modulating harmonic progression based on George Gershwin's "I Got Rhythm." The form AABA has 32 measures. Very popular during the Bebop era.

Riff: A short, repetitive motif which may be repeated unchanged or adapted to the chord changes.

Root Position Voicings (also: Spreads): Open position harmonies, voice lead, supported with the root in the bass voice.

Secondary Dominants: Any diatonic chord (except the VII) may be preceded by its own dominant chord. In addition to the *Primary Dominant (V7/I)*, five secondary dominants exist: V7/II, V7/III, V7/IV, V7/V, and V7/VI. They use diatonic chord scales with alterations for the chord tones.

Secundal Harmony: See *Cluster.*

Sequential Dominants (also known as Extended Dominants): Nondiatonic dominant chords that resolve to other nondiatonic chords such as another sequential dominant or its related II–7. There is an expectation to ultimately return to the diatonic.

Sequential Substitute Dominants: The tritone substitute chords for sequential dominants.

Side Slipping: Harmonic or melodic chromatic approaches.

Slash Chords: Triads (sometimes seventh chords) over bass notes are called slash chords because of their notation: a chord symbol followed by a diagonal slash and the name of the bass note, e.g., D/C.

There are two kinds of slash chords:

1) Inversions: F/A

2) Hybrids: Sometimes they may be analyzed as incomplete ninth, eleventh or thirteenth chords: G/C = Cmaj9 without 3rd. The G chord represents the upper structure of C (see *Upper Structure Triads*). Most often they are more complex like E/F.

Solo Break: An interuption of the rhythmic time flow, allowing one player to improvise.

Spread Voicings, Spreads: See *Root Position Voicings*.

Stoptime: The rhythm section reduces the accompaniment to the articulation of specific beats, usually in a repeated pattern.

Subdominant Minor Chords: Chords derived from IV minor: IV–7, IV–6, IV–(maj7); II–7(♭5); ♭VII7; ♭VImaj7, ♭VI6, ♭VI7; ♭IImaj7. See also *Modal Interchange*.

Substitute Dominants, subV, Tritone Substitution: A chord which may replace a dominant chord in a given harmonic progression. Every dominant seventh chord has a substitution with the same function. The root of the substitution chord is a tritone apart from the original one (tritone substitution). They have common tones (the 3rd and the 7th) and therefore share the same tritone, which defines – exchanged and enharmonically spelled – the dominant function.

Superimposition: A musical structure (chord, melody, rhythm) placed over another.

Synthetic Scales: Scales not historically developed but often created and used for special compositions.

Tag: A short repetitive musical idea at the end of a piece, or an arrangement.

Tensions, Options, Extensions: Harmonic color tones found by the continuation of building a chord in thirds above the 7th.

Possible tensions are: 9, ♭9, ♯9, 11, ♯11, 13, ♭13.

The altered fifth (♭5, ♯5) is sometimes considered as a tension (♯11, ♭13),

♭9 and ♯9 are only possible with dominant chords.

Diminished chords have four possible tensions: 9, 11, ♭13, maj7.

The function of each chord determines which tensions are possible.

Tertian Structures: Chords built by superimposing thirds. Compare: *Quartal, Quintal Harmony*.

Tetrad: A four-note cluster voicing.

Theme: A composition's melody.

Time: The rhythmic flow determined by a certain number of pulses.

Time Feel: See *Groove*.

Time Keeping: A rhythmic pattern which maintains the tempo, e.g., the cymbal played in quarter notes.

Trade, Trading Fours: To trade means to divide a chorus among soloists or between a soloist and the drummer. Each takes usually four bars (trading fours) in turn to solo over the form.

Transitional Harmony, Transient Tonality: A chord progression (often *sequential dominants* or *sequential substitute dominants*) in a functional context with no clear tonal center is called transitional. It may result in a modulation (transitional modulation) or just in a momentary instability of the given key center.

Transitional Modulation: See *Transitional Harmony*.

Tritone Substitution: See *Substitute Dominant.*

Turnaround, Turnback: Usually a two measure cadence with four chords at the end of a section or at the end of a chorus. The first chord usually has tonic function and the last one has dominant function. The turnaround leads back to the beginning of the chorus, to the next section, or repeats itself. In most cases the turnaround replaces the two-bar tonic chord at the end of the form to supply the static harmony and melody with an active chord progression.

Upper Structure Triads: Triads which are part of an extended chord structure and contain at least one tension.

Up Tempo: Fast; usually, metronome marking 220, or faster (per minute).

Vamp: A short (usually 2 or 4 chords), continually repeated, harmonic phrase.

Verse: The part of a tune with changing lyrics. In jazz the verse of a standard tune is most often omitted or used as introduction for the actual theme, the chorus.

Voicing: The actual position, or order of a chord's pitches. Voicings within an octave are called close voicings; open voicings exceed one octave.

Index

The Authors

Barrie Nettles

- Previously, Chairman – Core Music Studies, Harmony Department. Currently, professor – Harmony Department, Berklee College of Music, Boston, Massachusetts
- Studies – U.S. Navy School of Music, Arlington, Virginia
- U.S. Army Band of the Pacific, Honolulu, Hawaii
- Music therapist – State of Pennsylvania
- Arranging/composition studies – Berklee School/College of Music with Herb Pomeroy, Joe Viola, Phil Wilson
- Assistant to Executive Vice President – Frank Music Corp./Music Theatre International, New York City
- Professional performances/arranging – Steve Lawrence, Danny Thomas, Earl Grant, The Stylistics, Richie Cole, Charlie Mariano, Harvey Mason, Smokey Robinson and the Miracles, The 3 Degrees, Dave Stahl, Woody Herman

Richard Graf

- Guitarist and composer
- Assistant lecturer, studio/jazz guitar, University of Southern California, Los Angeles, California
- Studies – classical guitar and instrumental pedagogy at the University of Music and Performing Arts, Vienna, Austria; degree: Master of Arts, graduation Summa Cum Laude
- Jazz theory and jazz guitar studies – Berklee College of Music, Boston, Massachusetts
- Several awards in Austria and U.S.A.
- Professional performances/composing/arranging/producing – National Opera, National Theater/Vienna, Austria; Radio and TV commercials; several CDs; Solo CD "Rich Art;" performances in Europe and USA